To: Bert
Merry Christmas!
Love,
Ann + Howard

THE BALTIMORE ORIOLES

**MEMORIES AND
MEMORABILIA OF
THE LORDS OF BALTIMORE**

Text by Bruce Chadwick
Photography by David M. Spindel

ABBEVILLE PRESS · PUBLISHERS
New York · London · Paris

To Margie and Rory.
—B.C.

For all the fans who support my work.
—D.M.S.

EDITOR: Stephen Brewer
DESIGNERS: Virginia Pope and Patricia Fabricant
PRODUCTION EDITOR: Owen Dugan
PICTURE EDITOR: Kim Sullivan
PRODUCTION MANAGER: Lou Bilka

Compilation, including selection of text and images, copyright © 1995 Abbeville Press. Text copyright © 1995 Bruce Chadwick. Photography copyright © 1995 David Spindel. All rights reserved under international copyright conventions. No part of this book may be reproduced or utilized in any form or by any means, electronic or mechanical, including photocopying, recording, or by any information storage and retrieval system, without permission in writing from the publisher. Inquiries should be addressed to Abbeville Publishing Group, 488 Madison Avenue, New York, N.Y. 10022. The text of this book was set in Gill Sans. Printed and bound in Singapore.
First edition
10 9 8 7 6 5 4 3 2 1

Library of Congress Cataloging-in-Publication Data
Chadwick, Bruce.
    Baltimore Orioles: memories and memorabilia of the Lords of Baltimore / text by Bruce Chadwick: photography by David Spindel.
      p. cm.
    Includes bibliographical references and index.
    ISBN 1-55859-862-6
    1. Baltimore Orioles (Baseball team)—History. 2. Baltimore Orioles (Baseball team)—Collectibles. I. Spindel, David. II. Title.
GV875.B2C43   1995
796.357′64′097526—dc20   94-40596

Pages 2–3: The 1921 Orioles (see p. 47). **Title page:** A pin from the 1894 season (see p. 22) and a league patch from the 1950s (see p. 63). **Table of Contents** (clockwise from top): a reserved-seat ticket for an opening day gone by (see p. 45); an O's glove; the 1983 World Series trophy; an Orioles license plate (see p. 97); Cal Ripken, Jr. (see p. 108); the 1944 championship ring (see p. 56); an Orioles pennant; Boog Powell (see p. 83); a scowling Birds emblem (see p. 75); an O's alarm clock (see p. 65).

ACKNOWLEDGMENTS

We'd like to thank the collectors who let us into their homes to photograph memorabilia from the rich history of the Orioles, particularly Ted Paterson, Joe Bosley, and Steve Terman. We also extend our thanks to Greg Schwalenburg, historian and curator of the Babe Ruth Museum; to Josh Evans, president of Lelands, the New York sports auction house, for his assistance; and to the hardworking researchers at the National Baseball Hall of Fame in Cooperstown, New York, particularly its photo director, Patricia Kelly.

In addition we'd like to thank the staff of the Orioles for their help and cooperation, particularly media-relations director Rick Vaughn. Finally, we extend our special thanks to our editor, Stephen Brewer, and designer Virginia Pope, who worked with us on the book.

BRUCE CHADWICK AND DAVID M. SPINDEL

CONTENTS

ACKNOWLEDGMENTS • 7

INTRODUCTION
The Lords of Baltimore • 11

CHAPTER ONE
Baseball Comes to the Chesapeake
1855–1898 • 15

CHAPTER TWO
Ups and Downs
1899–1916 • 31

CHAPTER THREE
Kings of the Minors
1919–1953 • 47

CHAPTER FOUR
Back!
1954–1960 • 61

CHAPTER FIVE
To The Top!
1961–1965 • 73

CHAPTER SIX
The Glory Trail
1966–1979 • 81

CHAPTER SEVEN
Streaking Along
1980–1994 • 105

ORIOLES GREATS • 124

ORIOLES STATS • 130

AUTOGRAPH PAGE • 132

BIBLIOGRAPHY • 133

INDEX • 134

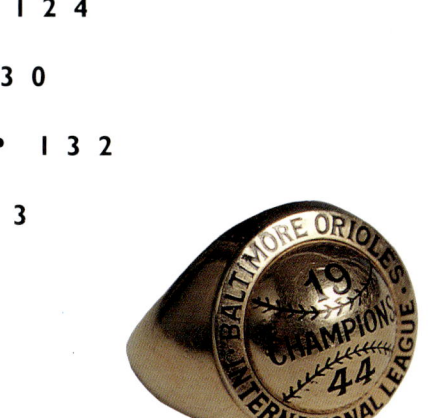

INTRODUCTION

THE LORDS OF BALTIMORE

Few American cities are as rich in baseball history as Baltimore. Young men first played baseball in Baltimore on amateur club teams in the early 1850s. The citizens of Baltimore, southerners in a border state that remained in the Union despite the presence of slavery, became even more interested in baseball during the Civil War, when Union troops occupied the city. Dozens of army units set up baseball teams, and their games—many played against local civilian teams—drew large crowds and gave baseball a permanent presence in the city.

The thirst for professional baseball has been strong from the earliest days of league play—from 1872, when Baltimore fielded a team in the first quasi-professional league, the National Association of Professional Baseball Players, to today, when a fine Orioles team plays in a beautiful new park, Camden Yards. Baltimore fans have seen their beloved Birds take nine minor-league championships, three National League pennants, four American League pennants, and two World Series.

Some of the best managers in baseball have toiled in Baltimore, among them Ned Hanlon, John McGraw, Jack Dunn, Paul Richards, Frank Robinson, and Earl Weaver. Dozens of the game's great stars have played for the Orioles over the years. In 1886 hurler Matt Kilroy struck out 505 batters.

This turn-of-the-century uniform, from Baltimore's Babe Ruth Museum, belonged to a team mascot who served as batboy.

INTRODUCTION

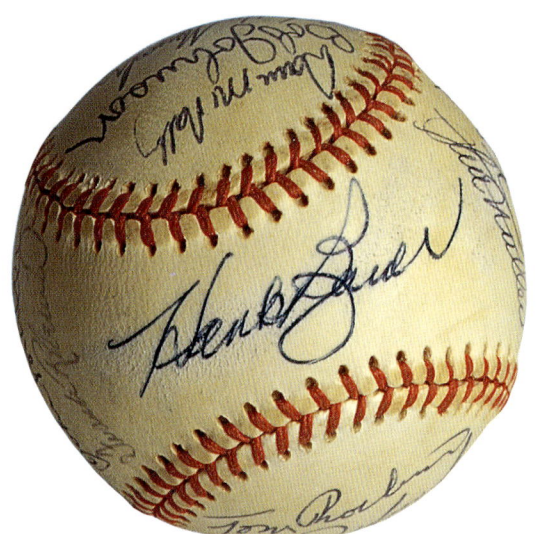

Manager Hank Bauer's signature is proudly displayed on a 1966 team ball.

The super team of the 1890s featured John McGraw, Wilbert Robinson, Hughie Jennings, Wee Willie Keeler, Dan Brouthers, and Kid Gleason. A raw kid named Babe Ruth signed with the Orioles in 1914. The teams of the 1920s starred George Earnshaw, Lefty Grove, and Jack Bentley, and they won seven International League pennants in a row with what is still considered to be one of the greatest teams of all time. The modern-era Birds have given fans the heroics of Frank and

Photo packs such as this one were popular with fans in the 1960s.

INTRODUCTION

The familiar number 22 belonged to Hall of Fame pitcher Jim Palmer, who won 268 games in his remarkable career.

October 1966 was a happy month in Baltimore—the Orioles swept the Dodgers in a four-game World Series.

Brooks Robinson, Milt Pappas, Boog Powell, Jim Palmer, Mark Belanger, Paul Blair, Mike Cuellar, Dave McNally, and Cal Ripken, Jr., the iron man who is expected to break Lou Gehrig's record for consecutive games one day soon.

For more than a century fans have flocked to see baseball wherever it has been played in Baltimore: in town parks, Bugle Field, tiny Oriole Park, mammoth Memorial Stadium. These days Orioles fans flock to Camden Yards, a brand-new stadium designed to look old and to take fans back in time—back through thousands of warm summer nights, back through a roster of some of baseball's greatest players, back through many years of baseball glory.

CHAPTER ONE

BASEBALL COMES TO THE CHESAPEAKE
1855–1898

No one is certain who threw the first pitch or hit the first ball in Baltimore baseball history. Baseball was thriving in Baltimore by 1855, though, just ten years after the first organized game of baseball was played at Elysian Fields in Hoboken, New Jersey. A dozen "gentlemen's" clubs fielded teams and played in city parks on weekends. The games drew thousands of fans. Baltimoreans were so crazy for the game that the Atlantics, a fabled semiprofessional team from New York City, made Baltimore their first stop when they set out on a barnstorming tour of the East Coast in the summer of 1860.

During the Civil War, Union troops moved into Baltimore with force after local citizens demonstrated pro-Confederate sentiments. With the troops came baseball, as the soldiers formed teams to pass the time. Baseball bloomed as hundreds of Baltimoreans flocked to games and began to play themselves. By 1867, more than twenty amateur clubs were playing in Baltimore. The National Association of Base Ball Players, which represented 237 amateur teams from coast to coast, elected a Baltimorean, Arthur Gorman, as its president. That group was superseded by the National Association of Professional Baseball Players, and in 1872 Baltimore entered the association with its first professional team, the Lord Baltimores. The Lords finished third their first season, but

The Orioles won the Temple Cup, the championship trophy of early baseball, in 1894, 1895, and 1896.

BASEBALL COMES TO THE CHESAPEAKE

Large "cabinet" cards showed early players, including members of the All America team that traveled to California with the Orioles for an off-season tour in the late 1890s. In 1872 an optimistic fan purchased a share of stock in the Baltimore Base Ball Club, which folded just two years later.

played like commoners after that. Fistfights interrupted most games the Lords played, and gambling among the players was rampant. The team wound up in the league cellar in 1874, and team officials, disgusted by the squad's behavior and its record, folded the team. The Lords were no more.

Several Baltimore teams played a semipro schedule throughout the 1870s. Baltimore was eager for pro baseball, though. In 1882, Harry Von Der Horst, a prosperous local brewer, sponsored a team in the new American Association. He named the team the Orioles, after the pretty bird that inhabits the Chesapeake Bay region. The association's six teams went head to head with the teams of the recently formed National League. The American Association knew the formula for success and thrived. In addition to Baltimore, the association placed teams in large cities where the National League did not play—Cincinnati, Louisville, Pittsburgh, Saint Louis, and the one exception to this rule, Philadelphia, which had a popular National League squad as well. The American Association charged twenty-five cents admission, compared to the National League's fifty cents; played on Sundays, which the National League did not; and, most important, sold beer, which the

BASEBALL COMES TO THE CHESAPEAKE

For brewer and team owner Harry Von Der Horst, baseball provided a lucrative demand for beer.

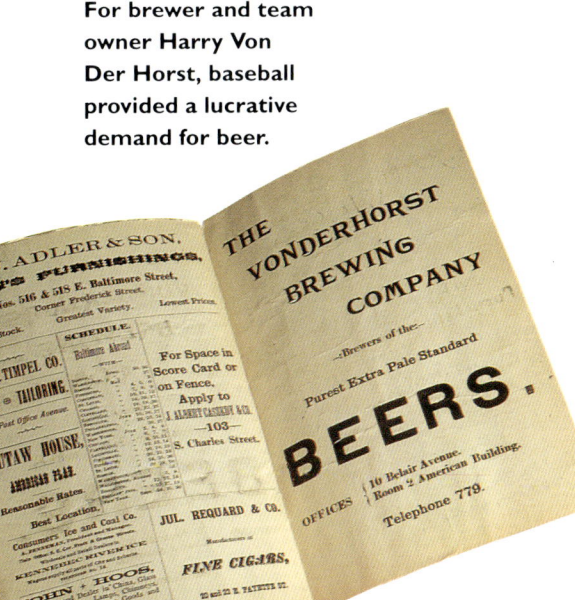

So many fans jammed old Oriole Park for the final game of the 1897 Temple Cup series that police had to put several thousand of them on the outfield grass.

National League forbade. At one point, when his team was doing badly, the portly, bewhiskered Von Der Horst stood in front of his brick-walled brewery, shrugged, and said, "Well, we don't win many baseball games, but we sell lots of beer."

Von Der Horst built Union Park, soon to be renamed Oriole Park, a wooden, six-thousand-seat ballpark at 25th Street and Greenmount Avenue, just off the well-traveled horsecar line. Union Park had a big picnic area, beer stands stocked with kegs of Von Der Horst's brew, and a large, clean restaurant that was packed before and after games. Von

BASEBALL COMES TO THE CHESAPEAKE

The 1889 ballclub finished fifth. Hurler Matt Kilroy (second from left, seated) won twenty-nine games, and first baseman Tommy Tucker (third from right, seated) led the league in hitting with a .372 average.

Der Horst and his general manager, feisty Billy Barnie, became the toast of Baltimore.

Even though the Orioles dawdled in last place, the team turned a hefty $30,000 a year profit. The Orioles gave fans some fine players in the 1880s. Matt Kilroy, a pitching wonder, set the all-time season strikeout record of 505. The pitcher's mound was then just fifty feet from home plate (it is now sixty feet, six inches), so Kilroy's record will probably never be broken. Another top hurler was John "Phenomenal" Smith, who won twenty-nine games in 1887. Oyster Burns hit .341 in 1887. First baseman Tom Tucker, later a star with the Boston Braves, hit .372 for the Orioles in 1889.

BASEBALL COMES TO THE CHESAPEAKE

Hughie Jennings slides into third base in an 1895 spring-training game against Detroit.

The business mettle of Von Der Horst and Barnie was tested for the first time in 1884, when the Union Association began to play ball in Baltimore and eleven other cities, including nearby Washington, D.C. The American Association met the new competition by placing new franchises in Washington and Richmond, Virginia. The Union Association was disorganized and underfinanced, though, and by the end of August seven of the twelve teams had folded; the league was gone after just one season.

However, more competition was waiting up the road. In 1890, players from the American Association and the National League, incensed over low salaries, fled to form the Players League. Von Der Horst, angry with the players who deserted him and with other American Association owners for not letting him play a role in setting league policy, left the association and put the Orioles in the Atlantic Association, a minor league. He changed his mind that August and came back to the American Association for the last few weeks of the season. But the American Association was doomed—hurt badly by competition from the Players League, which lasted just one season, the defection of the Orioles, and strong competition from the National League, the association stumbled through the 1891 season then folded.

In 1892, Von Der Horst and other owners of strong American Association teams merged with the National League, creating a twelve-team league. The Orioles finished dead last that first season in the National League, winning just forty-six games. At the end of the season, though, Ned Hanlon came on board as manager. Shrewdly trading for the fast, gutsy players he needed, Hanlon was to create for Baltimore one of the finest teams ever to trot onto a diamond.

BASEBALL COMES TO THE CHESAPEAKE

John McGraw, famed manager of the New York Giants, began his career with the Orioles.

Hanlon, who sported a thick mustache and short brown hair, was a stern taskmaster who would not let anybody interfere with his decisions, especially owner Von Der Horst. In fact, just to make it clear who was running the Orioles, Von Der Horst began sporting a button that read, "Ask Hanlon."

Hanlon began to clean house by threatening to trade scrappy, square-jawed infielder John McGraw. This threat made McGraw so angry that the nineteen-year-old turned into a hitting fool just to get back at the tough manager. Hanlon kept Wilbert Robinson, the big catcher who went seven-for-seven in one 1892 game, right where he was. He traded George Van Haltren, former manager and outfielder, to Pittsburgh for young Joe Kelley, also an outfielder, and, seeing potential in unformed young talent, grabbed Louisville shortstop Hughie Jennings, who was then hitting .148. On the advice of friends, Hanlon signed five minor leaguers, including pitcher Sadie McMahon and pitcher Crazy Schmit. He pulled off the trade of the decade in the winter of 1893 when he got hefty Big Dan Brouthers (six feet two inches tall, 205 pounds) and wispy Wee Willie Keeler (just five feet four inches and 135 pounds) from Brooklyn, where Brouthers was considered to be too big and Keeler too small.

BASEBALL COMES TO THE CHESAPEAKE

The 1890s produced the first "sketchbooks," souvenir booklets filled with statistics and illustrated with drawings.

Hanlon taught his squad how to play strategic baseball. He was the first to develop hit-and-run plays. McGraw would bat first and was almost always certain to get on base. Keeler would bat next, and McGraw would be well on his way to the next base before Keeler would inevitably punch a hit to right field. Hanlon also taught his players a pseudo bunt that quickly became known as the "Baltimore chop"—faking a bunt, the batter would smash the ball into the ground, making it bounce high in the air so he could beat the throw to first. Another Hanlon innovation was the cutoff play on steals—if there was a runner on third, the shortstop or pitcher would intercept the catcher's throw to second, nailing the runner at the plate or back at third.

After an eighth place finish in 1893, things started looking up for the Orioles. Everything worked. The new lineup that Hanlon unveiled on opening day of the 1894 season at Union Park included six future Hall of Famers (Brouthers, Keeler, McGraw, Jennings, Kelley, and Robinson) and two admirable pitchers: Kid Gleason, who would go on to manage the Chicago White Sox through five successful seasons, including the 1919 American League Championship, and Sadie McMahon, who won 138 games in five years. The Orioles dazzled their opponents. For the opening

doubleheader of the 1894 season, more than fifteen thousand fans packed six-thousand-seat Union Park to watch the O's crush the mighty New York Giants, 8–3 and 12–6, with an endless variety of hit-and-run plays, double steals, bunts, and chops. The Orioles swept the four-game series and moved on to mow down the rest of the National League. The fast, new, innovative "Baltimore baseball" so

BASEBALL COMES TO THE CHESAPEAKE

Pins commemorated the 1894 season, when the O's took their first National League pennant.

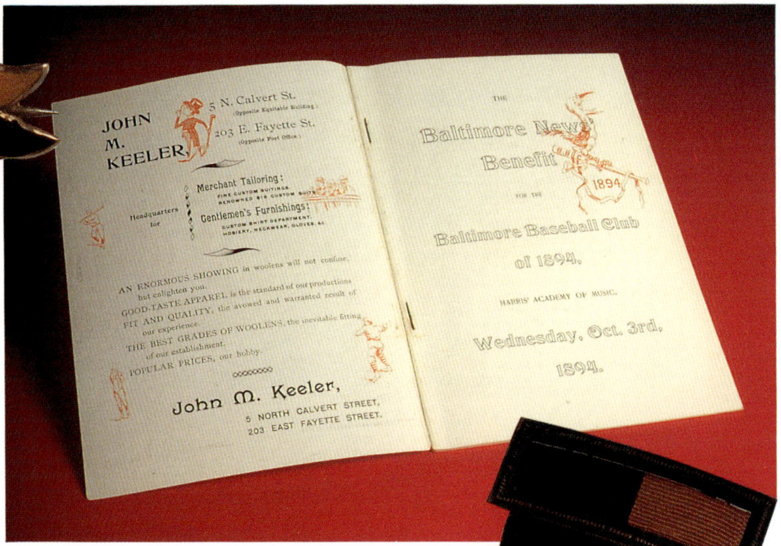

These lavish Orioles programs from the late 1890s are today much sought after by collectors.

Advertisers jumped at the chance to print their names next to the O's winning scores.

BASEBALL COMES TO THE CHESAPEAKE

The Orioles took the pennant again in 1895 and 1896.

infuriated opposing owners that they tried to have Hanlon's plays outlawed, to no avail.

The Orioles posted an 89–39 record and took their first National League pennant their first season under Hanlon. They won the pennant again in 1895 with an 87–43 mark and again in 1896 with a 90–39 record. Hanlon not only bred good players, but many of them, inculcated with his strategies, went on to become some of the game's great managers. Jennings, Robinson, and McGraw got into the Hall of Fame on the merit of their managerial achievements as much as for their batting averages.

Hanlon's boys played rough, too, and opposing owners and players, as well as umpires, complained bitterly about the Orioles' tactics. McGraw would often body block a runner coming into third or grab the shirt of a runner rounding third so he couldn't score. One day Pete Browning of St. Louis, unable to get out of McGraw's grasp as a ball rolled to the outfield fence, unbuckled his belt, let it fall into McGraw's grasp, and raced home holding his pants up. Other Orioles

23

BASEBALL COMES TO THE CHESAPEAKE

would stomp their spikes into the feet of catchers as they crossed the plate and deliberately bowl over basemen and fielders as they dove into a base. Orioles catchers would routinely throw their masks into the paths of runners trying to score. The O's would often take to the field with cut hands, broken fingers, and torn ligaments, enhancing their "macho" image.

Hanlon, not surprisingly, was every bit as devious as his players. He ordered the groundskeepers at Union Park to build up the dirt along the third-base line so his boys' bunts would always roll fair. He also had the grounds crew keep the outfield grass high, and it is said that he hid a dozen baseballs in the grass. If his boys could not get to a drive, they would simply pick up any of the hidden balls and throw it to second.

The *Sporting News* said that the

Emblazoned with photos of players and ads for beer, scorecards were as flamboyant as the team.

BASEBALL COMES TO THE CHESAPEAKE

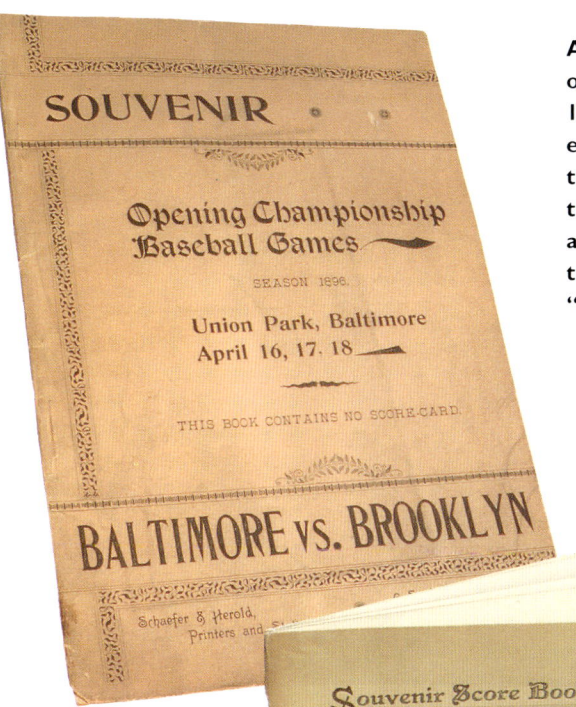

A program for the opening games of the 1896 season. By the end of that season, the Orioles had won three straight titles and fans considered the team to be their "old" champions.

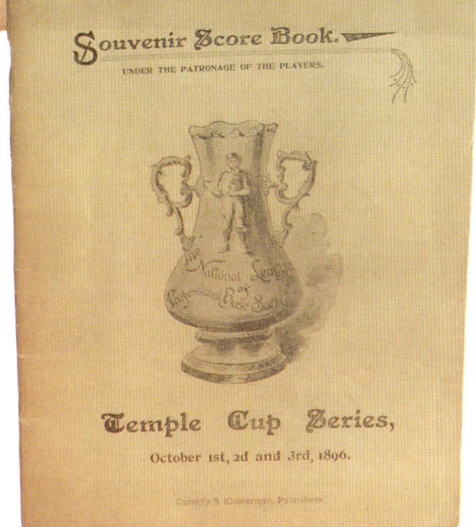

The Temple Cup series was the World Series of its day, played between first- and second-place finishers in the National League.

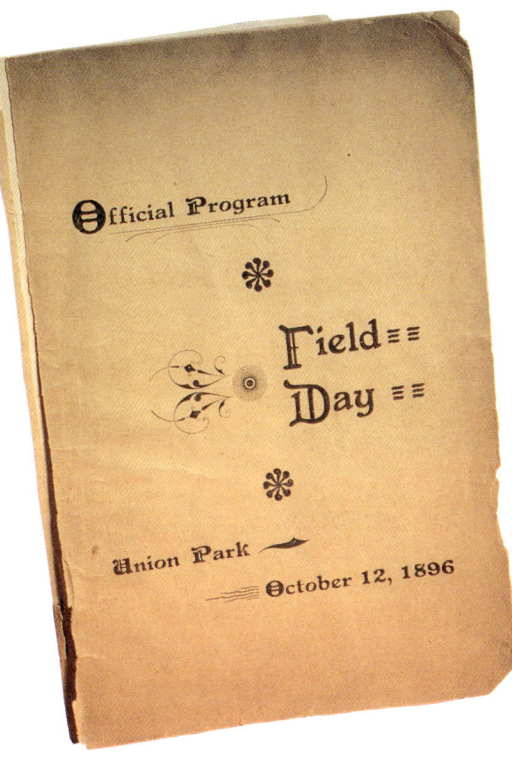

Field Day was a forerunner of Fan Appreciation Day.

BASEBALL COMES TO THE CHESAPEAKE

A team portrait of Baltimore's three-time champs showed the local heroes in their Sunday best.

BASEBALL COMES TO THE CHESAPEAKE

McGraw, front right, and his teammates comprised one of the roughest teams on the field, but they cleaned up for this formal portrait.

Orioles played "the dirtiest ball ever played in this country." Umpire John Heydler was even more critical. "They were mean, vicious, ready at any time to maim a rival player or an umpire if it helped their cause," he went on record as saying. "The club never was a constructive force in the game."

As much as the rest of baseball fumed at the Orioles, their fans loved them. Union Park was jammed for just about every game during the three straight years the Orioles won the pennant. Each player had his legion of followers. Big Dan Brouthers, stocky and fit, wearing a sporty handlebar moustache, was a favorite with fans, hitting .347 in the 1894 season. By 1896, his final year with the Orioles, he had a lifetime average of .342. McGraw, a tough-as-nails hitter who could spray singles to all fields, hit .340 in 1894. He was adored by his fans for his shirt-holding, tripping, and other pranks, and his inability to keep his mouth shut. He baited players (those on his own team as well as opposing squads) and umpires whenever he had the chance. He was a consistently good player and, with Keeler, won many a game with a fast hit-and-run play.

Wee Willie Keeler, a tiny, rail-thin batter, was the real marvel of the O's: He hit .361 in 1894, then .391, .386, .424, and .379 in the next four seasons, finishing with a lifetime average of .344. Once asked the secret to his sensational lifetime average, he replied, "Hit 'em where they ain't," a phrase that has become part of the American idiom. Wee Willie, who earned his Hall of Fame patch with Baltimore, was referring to his uncanny ability to place hits wherever he wanted them, using a

BASEBALL COMES TO THE CHESAPEAKE

Big Dan Brouthers was one of the great sluggers of turn-of-the-century baseball, finishing a 17-year career with a .343 average.

split-hand batting style that Ty Cobb later adopted. Keeler was also an able outfielder. In an 1897 game during the Temple Cup (a three-game post-season series between the National League's first- and second-place finishers) Keeler made the greatest catch in Orioles history. The center-field fence sloped backward at a forty-degree angle. To catch a home-run fly, Keeler ran halfway up the fence and caught the ball. His momentum carried him up and over the rest of the fence, and he fell down to a city street, startling passersby. Since Keeler still had the ball in his glove when he hit the sidewalk, the umpire ruled it an out.

Hanlon transformed red-haired, freckle-faced Hughie Jennings, who was so dreadful in his days with Louisville, from a .148 hitter into a slugger who hit .335 in 1894, .386 in 1895, and a dizzying .401 in 1896. The vocal, flamboyant Jennings wanted hits so badly that he often waited too long to duck on close pitches; he was hit forty-nine times in the 1896 season alone. He later became a fine manager, winning three pennants for Detroit.

Wilbert Robinson, the Orioles catcher, was one of the most durable men ever to play baseball. He once caught each game of a triple-header and then, the next day, caught both ends of a doubleheader. He and McGraw were close friends and

BASEBALL COMES TO THE CHESAPEAKE

The pennant-winning Orioles were cherished by every company in Baltimore.

Formal invitations and high hopes ushered in the 1897 season, but the Orioles were losing steam.

ran a pool hall together in the off-season. Robinson later took over as manager of the Brooklyn Dodgers, parting ways with McGraw, who was manager of the rival New York Giants. Joe Kelley, the least-publicized of the O's 1890s wrecking squad, was a sensational hitter who never hit less than .368 with Baltimore. He once went nine for nine in a doubleheader, and he scored 167 runs in 1894.

By the late 1890s, the Orioles were losing steam. They scraped through the 1898 season, finishing second, and finished third in the 1899. Fans, used to watching champions, started to stay home.

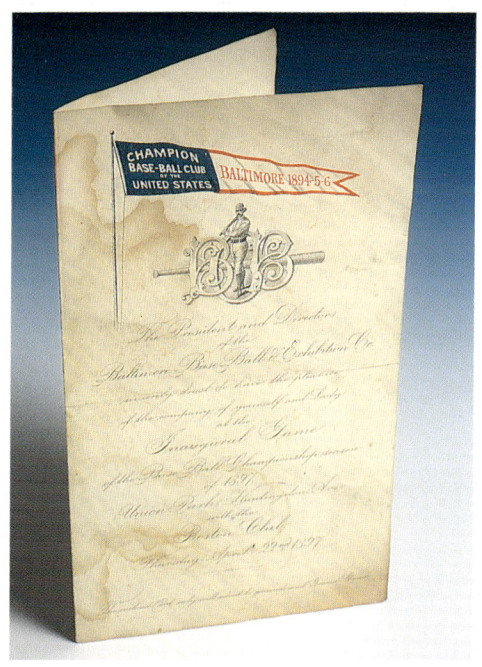

CHAPTER TWO

UPS AND DOWNS
1899–1916

During the heyday years of the mid-1890s, Harry Von Der Horst had formed a two-team syndicate with the Brooklyn Dodgers. By the end of the century, disgruntled with declining attendance at Oriole Park, he decided to direct his money and efforts to the Brooklyn Dodgers. Brooklyn had just become part of New York City, and it looked like baseball would be a financial bonanza there.

Von Der Horst made Ned Hanlon manager of the Dodgers and transferred his top players up to Brooklyn, including Wee Willie Keeler, Joe Kelley, Hugh Jennings, and half the pitching staff. Wilbert Robinson and John McGraw refused to go, preferring to stay with their beloved Orioles and the pool hall they ran together. After arguing long and loud with McGraw, Von Der Horst finally let him stay on with the O's as player-manager.

Hanlon and his carpetbaggers immediately began winning pennants for Brooklyn, in 1899 and again in 1900, creating the foundation for one of the most famous teams in baseball history. Meanwhile, the Orioles struggled to a fourth-place finish in 1899, just a game ahead of the Cards and Reds. John McGraw, who hit .390 himself, showed remarkable talent and did a brilliant job of managing—with few stars and despite a depleted squad, repeated arguments with Von Der Horst, and in midsummer the death of his wife.

The Orioles were losing steam when this photo of the 1899 team was snapped. The Orioles folded in the winter of 1900.

UPS AND DOWNS

Turn-of-the-century scorecards were made of thick cardboard and covered with advertising. By the time the Orioles traveled up to Brooklyn for the August 1907 games featured in the scorecard at right, they were part of the Eastern League.

The last year of the nineteenth century was also the last year for the Orioles. The Spanish-American War was putting a dent in ticket sales, and determined to be more profitable, National League owners dropped four of the twelve teams, trimming Baltimore, Washington, D.C., Cleveland, and Louisville. Baltimore fans were stunned: One summer they had one of the greatest teams in the short history of baseball, and just a few years later they had a vacant ballpark.

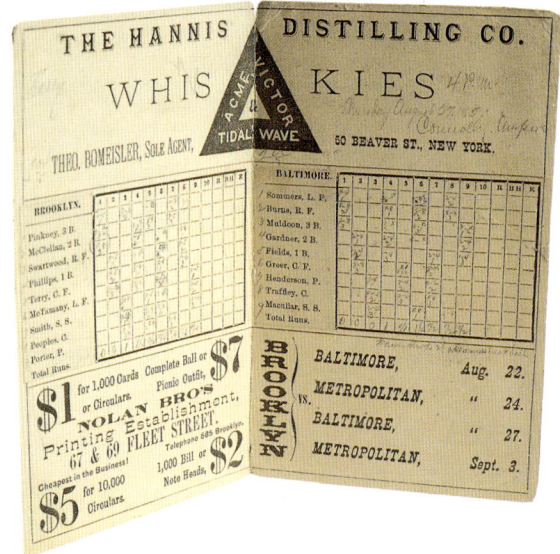

Baseball fans all over the country were chagrined that a city as large and important as Baltimore should not have a baseball team. At that time several owners in the defunct American Association were trying to regroup and start a new major league; they asked John McGraw and Wilbert Robinson to become managers and part owners of a new Baltimore club. Before the American Association could move into Baltimore, though, the Western Association, a minor league, began taking over teams to go into major-league ball with what would become known as the American League and made overtures to field a Baltimore team. Western Association chief Ban Johnson convinced McGraw and Robinson that his new league would

UPS AND DOWNS

be less of a risk than the American Association. Local businessmen Sidney Frank and Harry Goldman backed the Baltimore team, and in the spring of 1901 the Orioles came back to Baltimore—but not for long.

McGraw opened the season with a good team led by pitcher Joe "Iron Man" McGinnity, catcher Roger Bresnahan, pitcher-outfielder Cy Seymour, pitcher Jack Dunn, outfielder Mike Donlin, and, to please the fans, pitcher Crazy Schmit. The Orioles won their first two games, but began to stumble and finished fifth for their first season. The O's were plagued with problems that season, much of them having to do with the relationship between feisty John McGraw (the "Old Oriole") and league president Ban Johnson.

Johnson suspended McGraw the first time for spiking an umpire, then half a dozen other times for run-ins with other umpires, players, and fans. Johnson had Iron Man McGinnity tossed out of baseball for a month for spitting at an umpire. Six other players were booted out for a week or so at different times throughout

John McGraw was probably the best player to become a successful manager. He hit .334 lifetime and over .321 nine years in a row.

UPS AND DOWNS

Jack Dunn took over the Orioles in 1907 and ran the team as owner and manager until his death in 1928.

This wide-handled Orioles bat is typical of those used in the early days of baseball. It wasn't until the 1910s that Babe Ruth and other players discovered that a thin handle enabled them to put more speed on a hit.

UPS AND DOWNS

the summer. Things got worse in 1902. Determined not to give McGraw an inch, Johnson suspended him for five weeks in May for baiting an umpire. Then, on the very day McGraw returned, Johnson kicked him out for the rest of the season for arguing with another umpire. Furious, McGraw went up to New York and signed on as skipper of the struggling National League Giants, enraging everyone in the new American League. McGraw went on to become a baseball immortal with the Giants, who under his stewardship finished first or second in twenty-one of twenty-nine seasons.

During that same summer, Iron Man McGinnity, Roger Bresnahan, Joe Kelley, Cy Seymour, and some other Orioles also jumped ship to National League teams. By the Fourth of July, the rudderless O's had just fourteen players. They finished dead last for the 1902 season. Angry at the desertions and the drop in attendance and profits, Ban Johnson decided to move the Orioles to New York. There, they became the Highlanders, later the Yankees.

The Baltimore Premier Athletic Club was one of many semipro teams playing ball in baseball-crazy Maryland in the 1920s.

UPS AND DOWNS

Hugh Jennings, like John McGraw, was equally gifted as manager and player. He played on and off for seventeen years.

It was Ned Hanlon who returned baseball to his beloved Baltimore. Angry that the American League had dumped the Orioles, he bought a minor-league club in Montreal, part of the Eastern League, and moved it to town as the new Orioles. (The Eastern League became the International League, the strongest minor league in the United States, in 1911; Baltimore remained with the International League until the American League rolled back into town in 1954.) The team once again leased old, wooden Oriole Park, small but sturdy, and debuted to good crowds in 1903.

At first Hanlon put Wilbert Robinson in charge of the Birds. Still working as a catcher, Robbie did a creditable job but in the middle of the 1904 season was replaced by his old teammate Hughie Jennings, who had just earned his law degree from Cornell University. Jennings found himself with a good ball club and took to his job with great enthusiasm. While managing from the third-base coach's box, he would become so excited that he would wave his arms like a bird fluttering its wings, kick dirt with his left foot, and screech "EEEE yaaahhh!" at the top of his lungs. He also played shortstop, and, even at thirty-nine, he was a splendid batter. He was a terrific manager, too. His team finished a close second to Buffalo that 1904 season and almost had a pennant in 1905, but lost a close race by a single game to Providence, Rhode Island. In 1906, Jennings's final season, the Orioles finished third. Jennings's strategic moves and his ability to get along with players caught the eye of the brass on the Detroit

UPS AND DOWNS

Jack Dunn, famed as the manager of the Orioles when they were kings of the minor leagues, played for the team in 1902. A 1924 yearbook celebrates the success of the Orioles under Dunn.

Tigers, and they snatched him away from Hanlon. Jennings went on to lead the Tigers to three pennants.

Hanlon had been very impressed with the way the brilliant and flamboyant Providence manager, Jack Dunn, had steered his team through the tight, successful pennant struggle against Baltimore in 1905. Hanlon lured Dunn down to Baltimore, and right from the start fans and players loved tall, thin "Dunnie." He was eccentric, he had an uncanny ability to find and develop talent, and he won games. Perhaps the most amazing thing

about Dunnie was his high-pitched voice, which he used in an almost musical chant to encourage his own players, denigrate opposing teams, and humiliate umpires. It was said that you had never heard cursing until you heard cursing in that high-pitched, lyrical voice of his.

Born in Pennsylvania, Dunn began his baseball career pitching in New Jersey, started his minor-league career with Toronto, won the most games of his pitching career in New York (twenty-three for the Brooklyn Dodgers, in 1899), and started his career as a manager in Rhode Island. His only connection at all with Baltimore was a three-month stint as a pitcher with the Orioles in 1902, but like

Black Baseball in Baltimore

Roy Campanella got his start with the Baltimore Elite Giants, of the Negro Leagues.

Frank Robinson could not have found a more appropriate city in which to become baseball's first black Manager of the Year. Black baseball has a long, rich history in Baltimore, going back to 1874, when black teams played regularly at Newton Park and drew a cheering, integrated crowd.

The first professional black league, the League of Colored Baseball Clubs, was founded at a Baltimore hotel in 1887. The Lord Baltimores were the Baltimore entry in the league, which folded after a single season. Black baseball continued to thrive, though, and semipro teams played throughout the area. In 1920, after efforts to integrate the major leagues failed, a group of black teams banded together to form the Negro National League. A second circuit, the Eastern Colored League, was formed in 1923 and the Baltimore Black Sox became a member. The Sox played through the 1920s at Maryland Baseball Park, near the site of Westport Stadium. Thanks to the Black Sox, Baltimore made baseball history in 1926 when, in the Colored World Series, Atlantic City's Red Grier pitched the first perfect game ever pitched in a World Series, against the Black Sox at Maryland Baseball Park.

The powerful Elite Giants moved from Washington, D.C., to Baltimore in 1938. The Giants launched pitcher Joe Black, who went on to the Brooklyn Dodgers; infielder Junior Gilliam; and, best of all, teenage catcher Roy Campanella, who played in the

The Elite Giants were the other team in Baltimore until 1947, when baseball was integrated.

Negro Leagues for ten years before becoming a star with Brooklyn. The Elite Giants played their home games at Westport Stadium and at Bugle Field, where the outfield ran uphill to the fences. They won the Colored World Series in 1949 but folded the following year, as so many Negro League teams did after the game was finally integrated.

Charles Biot, who played for the Elite Giants from 1939 to 1941, says the team was more than a ball club. "We were the team of the black community of Baltimore," he remembers. "Times were hard for blacks then, with segregation, and the Giants brought blacks together as a family." The Giants also showed Baltimore great baseball. Joe Black, who went from the Giants to become major-league rookie of the year in 1952, remembers sitting with Campanella and making a list of truly outstanding players they had come up against with the Dodgers and with the Elite Giants. "We had six men on the Dodgers list," Black says, "and ten on the Giants list."

UPS AND DOWNS

so many other players, he left the team midseason for the Giants.

Dunn would become the savior of Baltimore baseball, as he transformed the Orioles into one of the most successful ball clubs, major or minor, of all time. Dunn and his family would keep pro baseball alive in Baltimore for fifty-three long years, until the modern-day Orioles finally took the field in 1954.

The Orioles finished a woeful sixth in 1907, Dunn's first season as manager, but bounced back the following year to win the first of the nine league championships they would garner under Dunn's leadership. Dunn, whom critics claimed still had the first nickel he earned, bought majority control of the Orioles from Hanlon in 1910, and sold a small piece of the team to the Philadelphia A's. Dunn

Baseball commissioner Kenesaw Mountain Landis brought the two greatest managers in the early history of the club, Jack Dunn, left, and John McGraw, right, together for a photographer in 1924 at Oriole Park.

UPS AND DOWNS

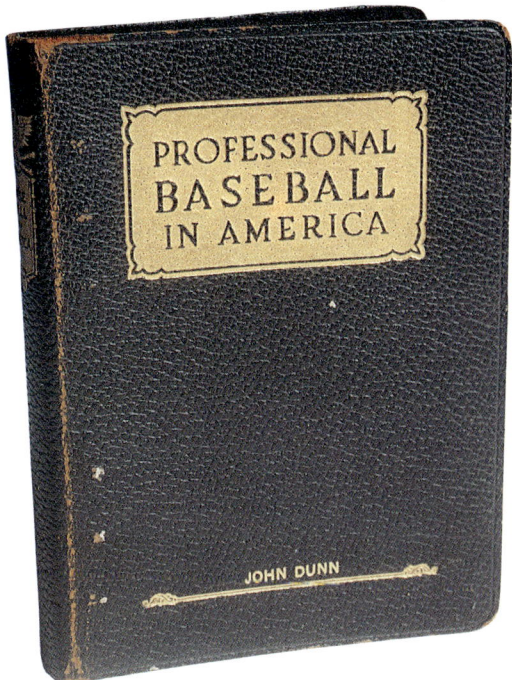

Dunn turned author to share his knowledge of the game in a popular book.

now had total control of the team and a pipeline to the A's, which would prove to be invaluable.

Although the Orioles did not take another pennant until 1919, they finished third in 1910, second in 1911, fourth in 1912, and third in 1913. Those same years, Philadelphia won three world championships, helped along by Dunn's shipment of talent to them and reception of discards from them. In 1910, Dunn sent Lefty Russell, who won twenty-four games for the Orioles in 1909, to the A's for $12,000, an impressive sum in those days, and got pitchers Rube Vickers and Jimmy Dygert in return. Vickers won fifty-seven games for Baltimore over the next two years. In 1912, Dunn sold A's manager Connie Mack his best two young outfielders, Eddie Murphy and Jimmy Walsh, even though Murphy had just won the International League batting title. The next year, Mack sent Dunn superstar pitcher Bob Shawkey, who, after two years in Baltimore, would later develop into a great hurler for the Yankees. Mack also sent pitcher-outfielder Cy Seymour, who had played for Baltimore back in John McGraw's managing days, back to town, and he sent down pitching ace Daring Dave Danforth. Dunn also sold Fritz Maisel to the Yankees and his brother, George, to the Browns, and the next season Fritz stole seventy-four bases for New York, earning the best stolen-base record in the majors.

Dunn prided himself on spotting good young ballplayers, and he made his wisest move—maybe the wisest move in the history of baseball—in 1914. A brother at a local Baltimore home for orphans and delinquents, St. Mary's, told Dunn he had an extraordinarily talented boy on his baseball team, a nineteen-year-old named George Herman Ruth. Dunn went down to a St. Mary's game and came away shaking. He had never seen anything like this kid with huge hands and a bigger-than-life personality. Ruth was the best pitcher Dunn had ever seen, and when

UPS AND DOWNS

The skinny kid on the far right is Babe Ruth, brought up to the minor-league Orioles in 1914. The O's later sold him to Boston for just $2,500.

UPS AND DOWNS

Ruth came up to bat, Dunn laid eyes on the best hitter he had ever seen.

Dunn wanted to sign George, known as "Babe" to his teammates, right away. The brothers insisted that Dunn "adopt" Babe Ruth, making him a legal ward of the Orioles until he turned twenty-one. He agreed, giving Ruth a $600 signing bonus and putting him on a train to spring training. There, this kid who had come out of nowhere turned those who saw him play on their ears and had sportswriters fishing for adjectives. Without breaking a sweat, in exhibition games Ruth routinely struck out Hall of Famers like Home Run Baker and Eddie Collins. Before spring training was half over, John McGraw, then managing the New York Giants, asked Dunn to sell Ruth to him. Dunn refused. He knew 1914 was going to be his year.

Babe Ruth or no Babe Ruth, the 1914 season almost saw the end of the Orioles once and for all. The scourge of the Orioles that season was the new Federal League and its major-league Baltimore team, the Terps. The Federal League came to be because a group of entrepreneurs, like the backers of several short-lived leagues before them, were convinced there was always room for another major league. Backed by millionaire businessmen, the Federal League fielded eight teams in 1914. Nowhere was the thirst for major-league baseball greater than it was in Baltimore, where fans were still smarting from having been abandoned by both the American and the National leagues. More than six hundred Baltimoreans chipped in to raise the $160,000 required to finance a team in the league.

The Terps built the much larger Federal League Park right across the street from Oriole Park. They ran extensive promotions and advertisements. They offered fans the chance to see major-league stars, and fans jammed the park. The Terps

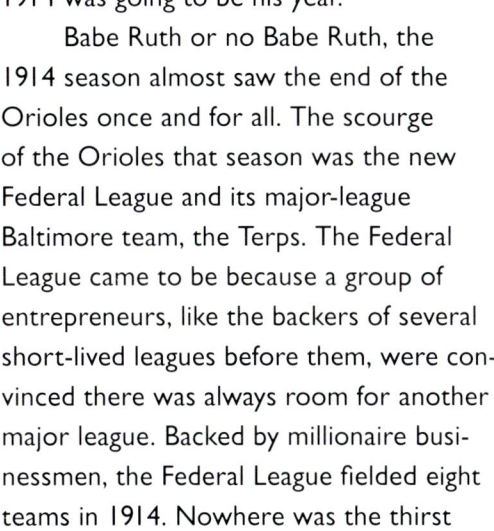

The Newark Peps played in the Federal League, which drove the American League and the Orioles out of town in 1914.

UPS AND DOWNS

This heavy wool uniform belonged to Fritz Maisel.

played well, too, finishing in third place the first year. Like the other teams in the new league, they stole players away from American and National League teams and brought promising players up from the minors. Otto Knabe, of the Phillies, became the Terps' manager, and shortstop Mickey Doolan and second baseman Runt Walsh also came over from the Phillies. The Terps got pitcher Jack Quinn and outfielders Guy Zinn from Boston and Benny Meyer from Brooklyn. They brought several players who had been sent down to the minors back up to the majors. Among them were pitchers "Piano Mover" Smith and "Kaiser" Wilhelm. Pitcher Jack Quinn won twenty-six games that year and George Suggs, another pitcher, took twenty-four.

The irony is, Baltimore didn't seem to notice the Orioles anymore, but they were a great team in 1914 and held a commanding first place in their league by midseason. The star of the team was young Babe Ruth, who caught everyone's attention right away when he shut out Buffalo in the season opener. He was 13–8 at midseason. The Terrapins immediately tried to woo Ruth away from the Orioles with an unprecedented deal that included a $10,000 signing bonus and a one-year, $10,000 contract. Dunn tripled Ruth's $600 a month salary to keep him, and the young pitcher raced around the streets of Baltimore on a bright red motorcycle he bought with his new fortune.

First place and Ruth's talents didn't help attendance, though. There was no drama left in the pennant race; with Ruth, the Orioles seemed to beat everybody.

UPS AND DOWNS

Check out the price of a reserved seat.

Crowds dwindled. Dunn, who just about owned the club himself, was on the verge of bankruptcy. To stay afloat, he started selling off players to major-league teams. Birdie Cree, the league's leading hitter, went to the Yankees for $5,000. One by one, off went the valuable players. Finally, in a last-ditch effort, Dunn reluctantly sold Babe Ruth to the Boston Red Sox for just $2,900 in what had to be the fire sale of the century. The money from the sales didn't help. Attendance plunged even more with Ruth gone.

Finally, Dunn left Baltimore to the Terps and moved his team to a new league, the Virginia League, and a new city, Richmond. His luck wasn't much better there, and he came back to Baltimore with the Orioles. He didn't go along with the plans laid by the American and National leagues to merge the Orioles with the Terps (paying Terps directors several hundred thousand dollars). He adamantly refused to run the new, combined, team. He didn't want to merge with another team, especially the team that had forced him to flee to Virginia. He decided to fight to run the Orioles independently.

The dispute evolved into the most important lawsuit in the history of American sport. The directors of the Terps sued the American and National leagues, charging that they behaved as business

monopolies and that their actions were in violation of the Sherman Anti-Trust Act. The case kicked around the courts for six long years. In 1922 the U.S. Supreme Court ruled in favor of the major leagues. In a majority decision written by Justice Oliver Wendell Holmes, the high court ruled that baseball was a sport, not a business, and was exempt from any laws involving business monopolies. That decision, brought about by Baltimore baseball, legalized the reserve clause, which bound players to their teams, and freed clubs of the legal restrictions that bind all other American businesses.

CHAPTER THREE

KINGS OF THE MINORS
1919–1953

Jack Dunn was not overly enthusiastic about his return to Baltimore. He had been forced to sell Babe Ruth, his major gate attraction. He had lost his fans to the Terps. And he was convinced that Baltimoreans, after seeing the American, National, and Federal leagues come and go, were fed up with baseball.

Dunn was wrong. In a way, the collapse of the Federal League jolted baseball fans into realizing that major-league ball just wasn't going to come to Baltimore, and that they would be better off supporting their Orioles. Dunnie was amazed to see fans turn out in droves to welcome the returning Orioles. He was just as amazed when the Terps, involved in bitter litigation with the major leagues, offered to sell him Federal League Park, a much larger and safer stadium than old, wooden Oriole Park, at a good price. Dunnie renamed the new stadium Oriole Park, and the old one was eventually knocked down. Dunnie's team, though hurt by the sales of players, was still pretty good, and the Orioles put on a good show. They finished fourth in the International League in 1916 and third in 1917 and 1918.

World War I helped the Orioles considerably. Most of the major-league stars went off to fight in Europe, and their teams had to turn to the minors to fill out their rosters. Most turned to Dunn, the man who

Maryland fans swore that the 1921 Orioles, who won a third-straight International League pennant, could beat any major-league team in the nation.

A woodcarver rendered this statuette of an Oriole.

over the past decade had developed so many fine ballplayers and sold them to the majors. Dunn had talent and he had a price. The majors met it.

The war opened the eyes of minor-league owners to their worth. Their teams in major cities like Baltimore and Syracuse, New York, drew crowds as large as the major-league teams did, and minor-league heroes were as big in their towns as major-league stars were in theirs. The minor leagues then had an agreement with the major leagues that any player who had been drafted by the majors before playing for a minor-league club had to be sold to the drafting club for $7,500, any time the big-league club wanted him. As a result, the minors regularly lost stars and good gate attractions for little compensation.

In 1919, officials of leagues in the minor-leagues voted to throw out the old draft rule. For minor-league owners, the vote was a move toward independence and a chance to make more money selling players to the majors. Dunn realized this was his chance to find, develop, and keep talent, building a dynasty, and that is just what he did. He was now free to keep his best players and bring up the young stars he and his scouts found without fear the majors would snatch them away.

In 1919, the first year the draft rule was dropped, Dunn won one hundred

KINGS OF THE MINORS

Third-baseman Fritz Maisel joined the Orioles in 1917, **after an impressive six-year career with the Yankees.**

games and the International League pennant. He then won seven straight flags, almost all by wide margins, taking a hundred or more games every year—a then-record 119 games in 1921, 115 in 1922, and 117 in 1924. The Orioles won the pennant by ten games or more in four of the seven years. Strangely, the Birds did not play that well in the year-end Junior World Series, which matched the International League champs against the American Association champs, taking just three of the six series.

The Orioles certainly gave fans their money's worth, though, producing such fine players as Joe Boley, Fritz Maisel, Otis Lawrey, John Honig, Ben Egan, Socks Siebold, George Earnshaw, and Johnny Ogden. And then there were the stars. Pitcher Jack Bentley was supposed to be the majors' next Babe Ruth. He was 41–5 in his 1920, 1921, and 1922 seasons with the Orioles and consistently hit over .330. In 1921 he hit .412, playing regularly. Dunn sold Bentley, in 1923, to the New York Giants, where the pitcher started out well (13–8 on the mound, .427 at the plate in 89 at-bats) but faded after a few seasons. Max Bishop was one of the International League's best second basemen and hitters. He went on to great success with the Philadelphia Athletics, hitting .271 lifetime and leading the American League in fielding four times.

KINGS OF THE MINORS

Various groups honored the O's at the start of each season.

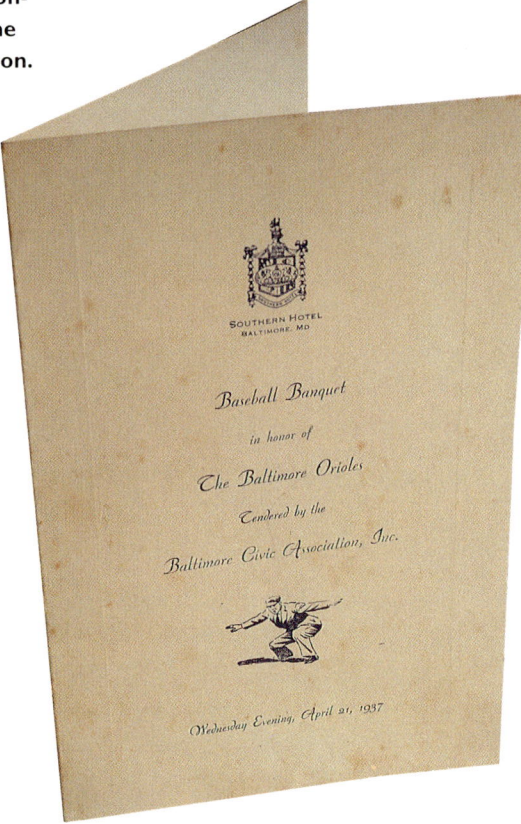

We were good because Jack Dunn just let us play baseball. He didn't pull pitchers. He stuck with them. We didn't even have signals. If you had a 3-count, he'd tell you to use your judgment and wing at the next one if it was good. If you thought you could steal, you stole. You didn't look for his decision. It was a team built on instinct, ballplayer instinct, and that helped us win.

—TOMMY THOMAS,
PITCHER IN THE 1920s, MANAGER IN THE 1940s

Then there was Lefty Groves. The name of this tall, string-bean-thin southpaw hurler was really Lefty Grove, but somewhere along the line in his rookie days he signed his name with an "s" and he was known as "Groves" ever since. Lefty was the greatest pitcher in the history of the minor leagues. He pitched four and a half years for the Orioles, winning 108 games and losing just 36. He was a strikeout artist with no equal, fanning 1,118 in four seasons and 330 in 1923 alone. By the middle of that season he was the talk of the country. Several major-league teams wanted him, and Groves wanted to move up. Dunn did not want to sell his great star and number-one gate attraction. He waited and waited and waited, repeatedly denying Lefty his chance to go to the majors. Finally, in 1926, the Philadelphia A's offered $100,000 for the mound ace, and Dunn relented. From the sale of Groves, Jack Bentley, Max Bishop, and other top players Dunn made enough money to keep the Orioles solvent forever.

The sale of stars hurt the team, though, and the Orioles tumbled to fifth in 1927. The next year, Dunn died of a heart attack at age fifty-eight, bringing an era to an end. Without their leader and visionary, the Orioles stumbled through season after season, finishing near the bottom in nine of the next eighteen years and never

KINGS OF THE MINORS

The great Lefty Groves was sold to the Philadelphia A's in 1926 for the then-record price of $100,001—the extra dollar topped what the Yankees paid the Red Sox for Babe Ruth.

The 1921 O's brought Baltimore its third straight International League Championship.

KINGS OF THE MINORS

The Orioles issued an official pin each season, and loyal fans sported them as part of their summer attire.

Pennants sold briskly at Oriole Park in the 1944 championship season.

winning another pennant. The Orioles did have their moments, though, and the best was in 1930, when Joe Hauser hit sixty-three home runs. In 1932, Buzz Arlett hit fifty-four homers, batted .322, and drove in 141 runs. He hit four home runs in one game—not once, but twice, in one month!

In 1944, a team of relative unknowns put together a miracle season of come-from-behind victories. They took the International League pennant and won the Junior World Series. The trophies were important, but the 1944 championship

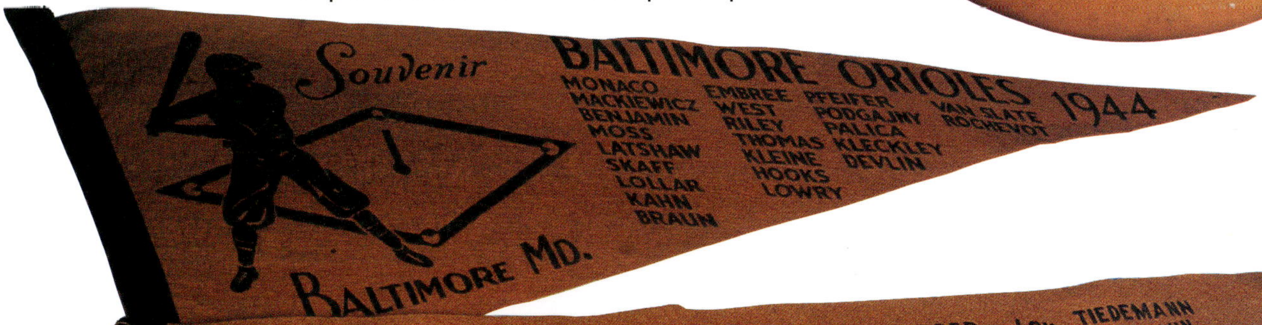

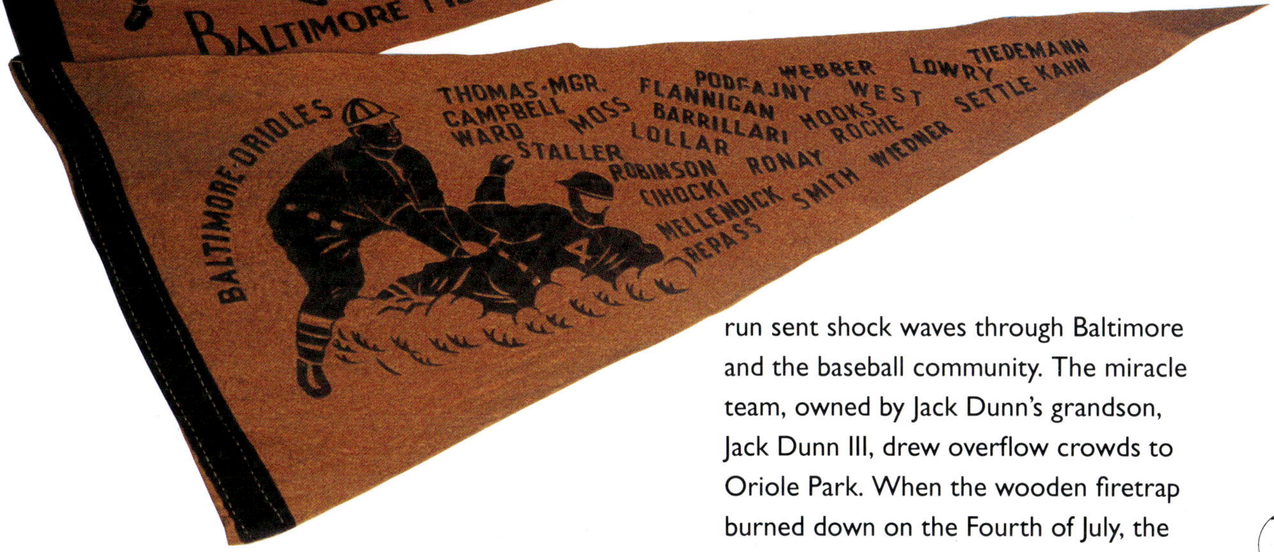

run sent shock waves through Baltimore and the baseball community. The miracle team, owned by Jack Dunn's grandson, Jack Dunn III, drew overflow crowds to Oriole Park. When the wooden firetrap burned down on the Fourth of July, the

53

KINGS OF THE MINORS

BALTIMORE "ORIOLES" - 1944

The minor-league Orioles, so powerful in the early 1920s, returned to top form in the mid-1940s.

O's leased Municipal Stadium, built for football, and refitted it for baseball. Municipal could hold huge crowds, and crowds of forty thousand and more flocked to the stadium for league playoffs. During the Junior World Series against the Louisville Colonels, one of the games at Municipal pulled 52,833, with an additional 10,000 standing, an International League record. Ironically, 21,000 fewer

KINGS OF THE MINORS

A fan kept these newspaper clips about Oriole Park before and after the 1944 fire.

The fire leveled old Oriole Park.

KINGS OF THE MINORS

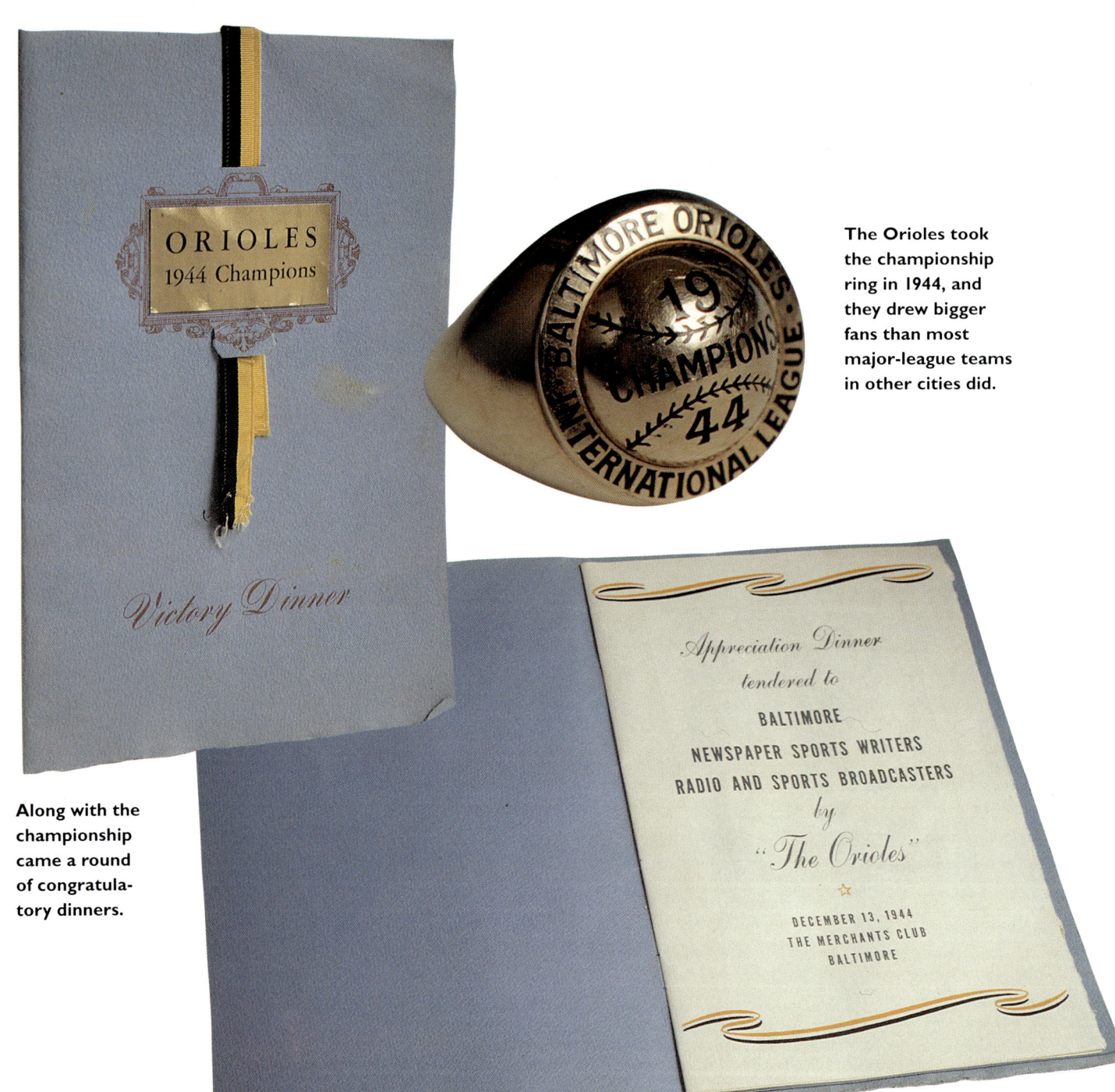

The Orioles took the championship ring in 1944, and they drew bigger fans than most major-league teams in other cities did.

Along with the championship came a round of congratulatory dinners.

KINGS OF THE MINORS

After the 1944 championship, consistently good baseball, expanding radio coverage, and such civic events as rallies kept momentum for a major-league return to Baltimore running high.

fans attended a World Series game played in Saint Louis that same day.

The major leagues, realizing that Baltimore had a bigger fan base than just about any major-league city, began considering putting one of their franchises there. Baltimoreans became convinced that they

KINGS OF THE MINORS

In the late 1940s beer ads still adorned Orioles' programs, just as they did in the late 1800s under Harry Von Der Horst.

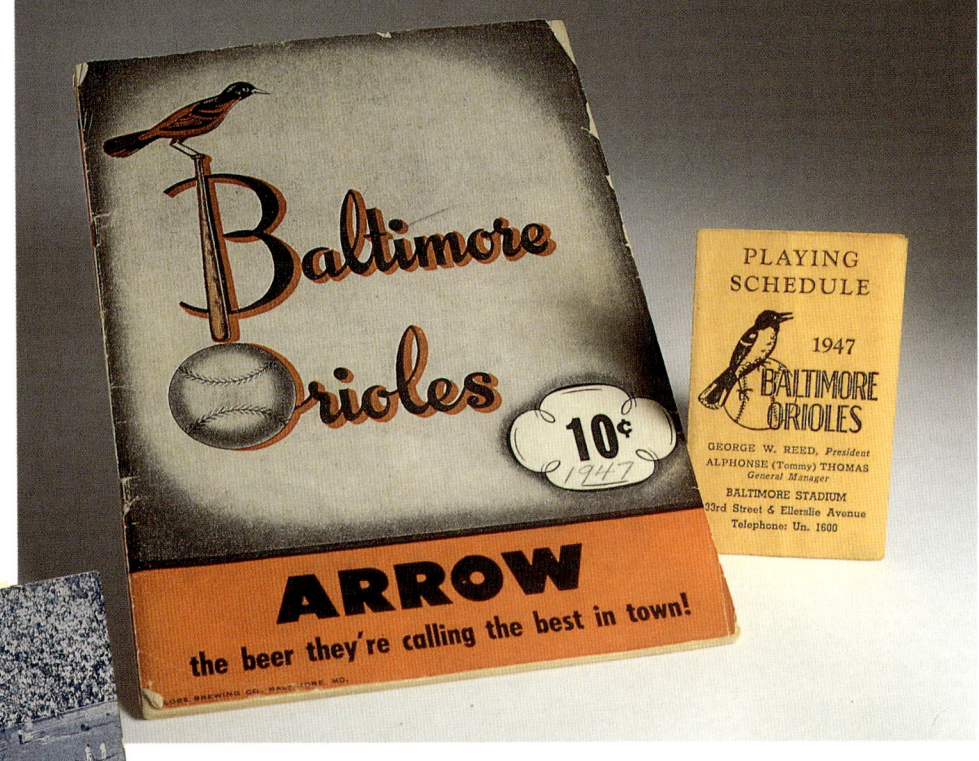

should have a major-league team. Everyone joined the campaign. Public officials began lobbying for a team. Roger Pippen, columnist for the now-defunct *News-Post,* spearheaded a campaign to rebuild Municipal Stadium so it would be more attractive to the majors.

Lou Perini, owner of the Boston Braves, considered moving his team to Baltimore in 1949, but the deal fell through. Bill Veeck tried to move his Saint Louis Browns to Baltimore in 1952, but the

KINGS OF THE MINORS

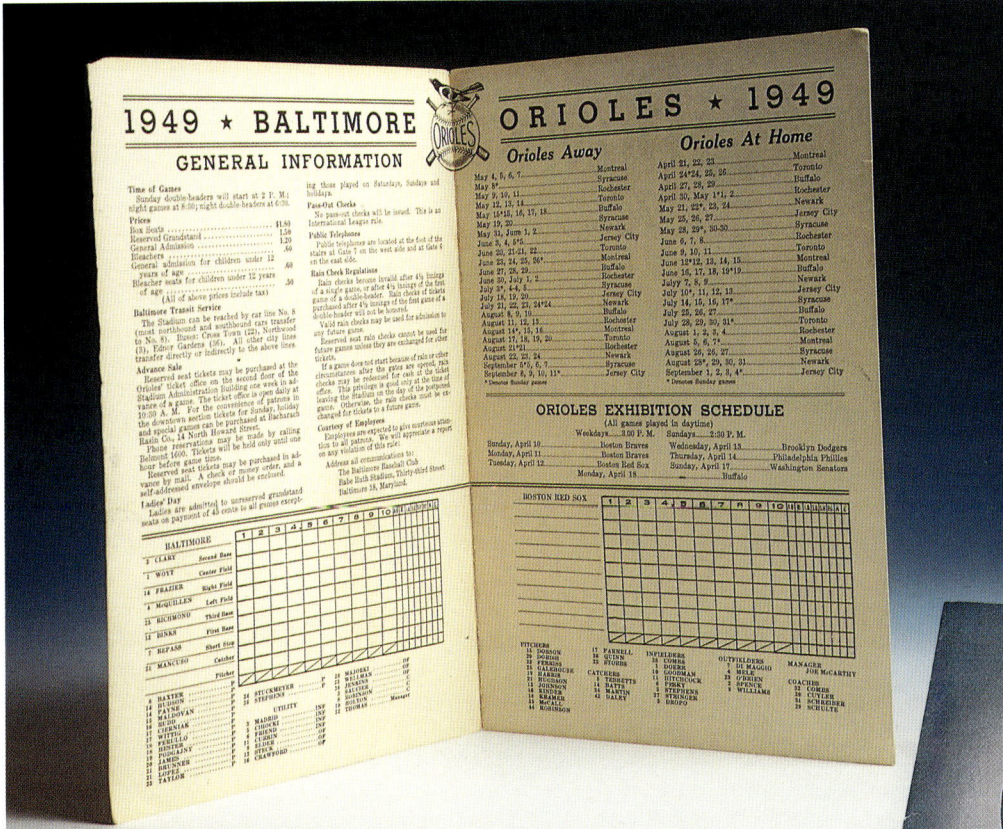

Chances for a major-league comeback were looking pretty handsome, too, as the 1940s ended with solid scores and deals for a franchise were in the works.

American League blocked him, demanding that the team be locally owned. The majors okayed the move when Veeck sold out his interest in the Browns to a Baltimore group headed by lawyer Clarence Miles. The transplanted team bought out the Dunn family's interest in the minor-league Orioles and prepared to unveil the spanking new Baltimore Orioles in the spring of 1954.

CHAPTER FOUR

BACK!
1954–1960

The parade celebrating the new Baltimore Orioles on the opening day of the 1954 season was one of the most heavily attended events in Maryland history. More than a million people lined the streets, packed six and seven deep for more than three miles. City workers were given half the day off. Schools were closed. The new Orioles rode through town in open cars, throwing plastic baseballs to their fans. Vice President Richard Nixon, who tossed out the first ball, also rode in the parade, as did American League president Will Harridge; Connie Mack of the Philadelphia A's and Clark Griffith of the Washington Senators, the two oldest managers in baseball; Jack Doyle and Boileryard Clarke, the only two surviving members of the 1890s wonder team; and to top it all off, the widow of John McGraw.

The capacity crowd at the ballpark was just as enthusiastic as the throngs in the street. As each new Oriole was introduced he was greeted with a deafening roar of approval. To Baltimore baseball fans, it did not matter that their new Orioles had been a last-place team the previous season. It did not matter that they were not only a last-place team but a last-place team that lost a whopping one hundred games in 1953. It did not matter that the team had no superstars, or that the new first baseman was the fabled Eddie Waitkus, who had been shot and nearly killed

All of Baltimore celebrated when the American League announced it would bring the St. Louis Browns franchise to town.

B A C K !

They're back! Baltimore fans greeted their once-again-major-league Orioles with a sustained ovation following a morning-long parade through the city.

It did not require too much coaxing to get fans to order tickets to see the new major-league Orioles.

The team went all out in 1954, with schedules, yearbooks, flyers, and programs.

BACK!

Fans wore team patches proudly in the 1950s.

We were thrilled to get out of St. Louis and into Baltimore. We were a last place team in St. Louis and, at the end, we were only drawing 1,500 or so people a game. It's hard to give your best in an empty stadium. When we got to Baltimore, we found the people didn't care that we were a last place team. We were their team and they loved us. That whole year I was treated like the pitcher who won the World Series just because I was a Baltimore Oriole. I played on World Series champs later, with the Yankees, and playing for the Orioles that first year was the same as playing in the World Series for the Yankees. I never saw such great fans in my life.

—BOB TURLEY,
WHO WAS 13–14 FOR THE ORIOLES IN 1954

in a Chicago hotel room by a woman he did not know (the incident inspired the novel and film, *The Natural*). All that mattered was that the Baltimore Orioles were, after fifty-two years, back in the major leagues.

The crowd yelled even louder that afternoon when Vern Stephens and Clint Courtney socked home runs, and the O's defeated the White Sox 3–1 on the mercurial arm of fastballer Bob Turley. The cheering soon subsided, though. By midseason the team had stopped winning and began to slide badly, losing one hundred games for the season. One problem was the size of Memorial Stadium. It was just too spacious for power hitters (the center-field hedges were a long 450 feet from home plate), and all those long fly balls the O's hit became nothing but big outs.

Attendance was strong all year, though, and on the last weekend of the season at-home attendance shot over the

Memorial Stadium, rendered here with an Art Deco look, was home to the Birds for almost four decades.

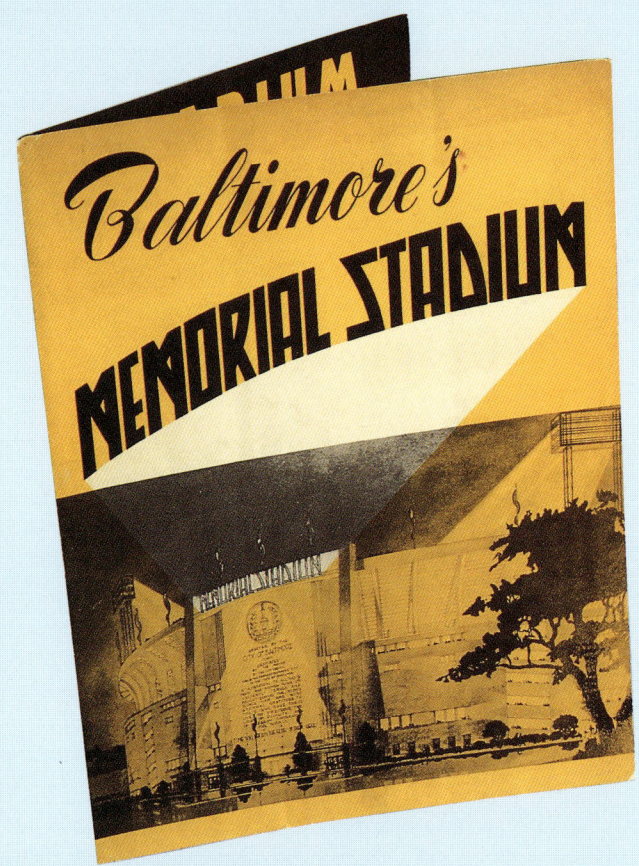

I'll never forget the 1954 Opening Day parade as long as I live. It was an explosion of joy by the people of Baltimore. They were a major American city with only minor league ball for 50 years. They knew they deserved a major league team. Everybody knew it. In '54, they finally got one. They loved us to death. The same thing happened in 1993 in Miami and Denver. Given a chance to show they were major league cities, both areas, which had strong minor league teams for decades, produced record crowds.

—CAL ABRAMS,
WHO PLAYED ON THE 1954 BALTIMORE TEAM

B A C K !

Manager-owner Paul Richards made the Orioles a winning team and became a national hero himself.

Clocks were among the memorabilia the major-league O's inspired in the 1950s.

one million mark—the season final was 1,060,910. On the field the Orioles had their moments in 1954, winning some thrilling games, some squeakers, and some they had no business winning. Some of the players did well. Bob Kennedy hit a grand slam on July 30. Cal Abrams, thought to be well past his peak, got hot in midsummer and wound up hitting .283.

Fans fell in love with their new team, win or lose. The front office was not about to keep losing a hundred games a season, though. After all, there was grand Oriole tradition to uphold: nine major-league pennants, three straight National League pennants with the 1890s wonder team, and the ghosts of John McGraw and other great Orioles. The owners hired Paul Richards, the bold and innovative manager of the Chicago White Sox, as general manager to turn the fortunes of the Orioles around.

Richards had won several flags for minor-league teams he had managed, and the struggling White Sox had made him manager in 1951. Known for his dabbling and innovating, in the winter of 1954 Richards had engineered an eighteen-player trade with the Yankees. Under Richards, the Orioles got better, but only slowly. The players found themselves being moved from bench to field and back again and from one position to another.

BACK!

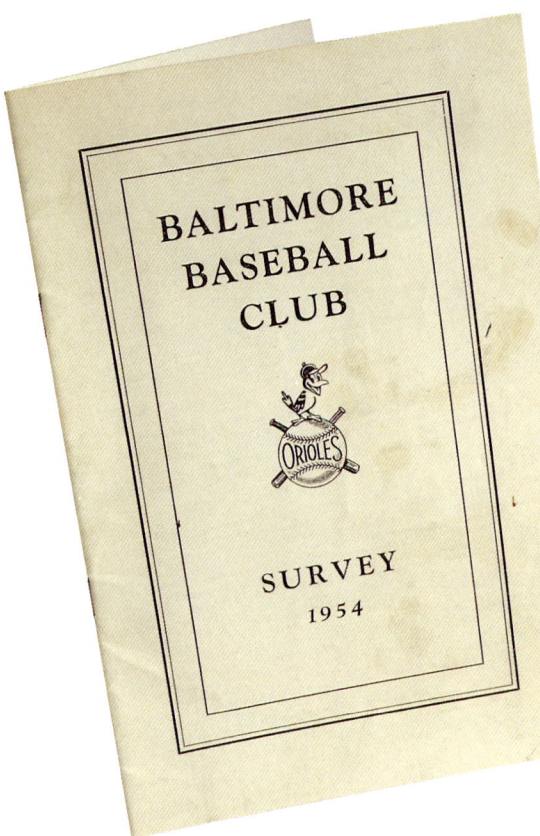

The results of this survey, taken in 1954, convinced the American League that Baltimore was prime turf for a franchise.

Altogether, fifty-four players appeared on the field for the Orioles that year. Ten men played third base. None of the maneuvers helped as the team floundered. Attendance plunged and fan interest waned as the losses mounted. The Orioles even lost to their York, Pennsylvania, farm team that season, by 13–1. By October they had

A boyish Brooks Robinson, right, at spring training. Boog Powell, left, and Robinson were a lethal combination in the 1960s. Robinson hit 268 homers and Powell hit 339.

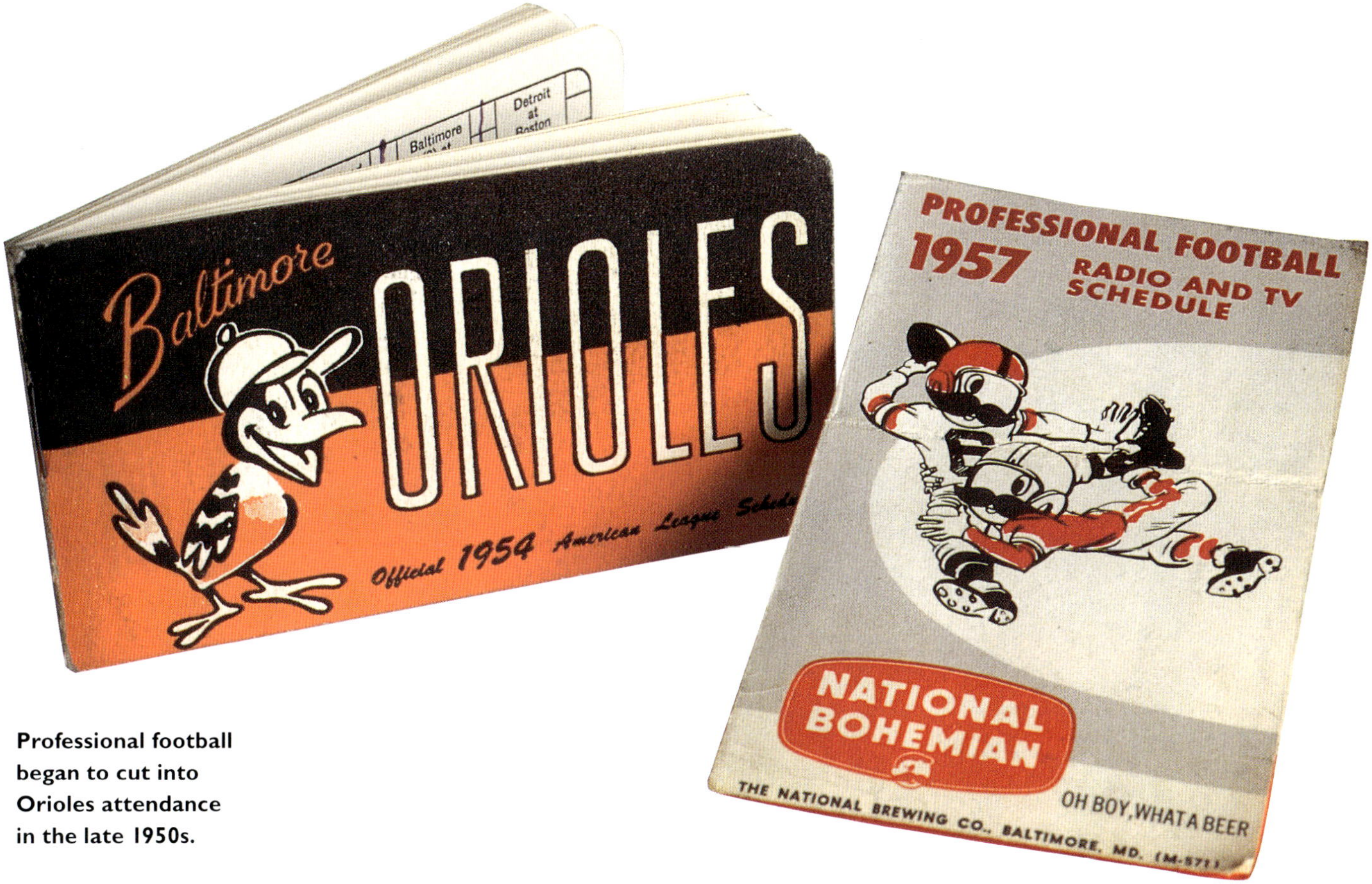

BACK!

Professional football began to cut into Orioles attendance in the late 1950s.

dropped another ninety-seven games and finished in seventh, ahead of only the lowly Washington Senators.

There was some improvement the next year as the Orioles moved up to sixth place. Richards was busy signing promising young players and making trades. One of his finds was a skinny kid from Arkansas who couldn't run, couldn't hit, and could barely throw, but who Richards liked on instinct. His name was Brooks Robinson. For the 1956 season,

Richards's trades brought in Bob Nieman, George Kell, Connie Johnson, and Mike Fornieles. They helped. Nieman hit .320 for the season, fourth highest in the league. Kell played so well he made the All-Star team, the first Oriole ever to do so. Nieman also hit safely in twenty consecutive games, a club record. Catcher Gus Triandos drove in eighty-eight runs that season. On the mound, Ray Moore, from nearby Upper Marlboro, Maryland, had a respectable 12–7 season. There

BACK!

The Orioles were serious contenders for the pennant in 1957 and again in 1958.

was tragic loss when catcher Tom Gastall drowned after his plane went down in Chesapeake Bay. All told, the Birds won more than they lost at home, cheering their fans a bit.

The Orioles inched up in the standings again in 1957, finishing fifth despite a dreadfully slow start that kept them in seventh for much of the first half of the season. They finally reached equilibrium, winning seventy-six and losing seventy-six, and they gave fans a tough, never-say-die team. Even Casey Stengel, the irascible skipper of the Yankees, was impressed by the tenacity of the Orioles. "They play every game like it's the World Series," he said. Bob Boyd hit .318, fourth in the league, and Billy Gardner had 169 hits, a team record. The fleet-footed O's were second in the league in bases stolen, with fifty-seven. Fans responded to the improvement, and the one million attendance mark was broken again.

The 1958 season was a watershed for the Orioles. Gus Triandos became a power-hitting catcher, slamming thirty home runs. Baltimore landed the All-Star

BACK!

game, and the American League won it behind the pitching of the O's Billy O'Dell. Rookie pitcher Milt Pappas arrived that year and finished with a respectable 10–10 record. Hoyt Wilhelm, the dazzling knuckleballer, tossed a no-hitter. The O's beat the Yanks in a doubleheader. Pitcher Arnold Portocarrero won fourteen games. The Orioles wound up in sixth place, but for two months were in fourth and

Baltimore landed the All-Star game in 1958, fanning the flames and helping to build attendance.

B A C K !

In the 1950s, the jaunty bird became an oft-seen public figure in Baltimore.7

seriously threatened third. At the end of the year, new president Lee MacPhail arrived. Paul Richards had done wonders for the Orioles, bringing them within the shadows of the top. MacPhail would push them closer.

The son of Larry MacPhail, who brought pennants to Cincinnati and Brooklyn, Lee MacPhail served as director of player development for the Yankees from 1948 to 1958. He scouted and developed dozens of ballplayers who became great players for the Bronx Bombers. Arriving in Baltimore, MacPhail was convinced the Orioles could win the pennant; they just needed a push. He was good at providing pushes. Looking for young talent to build a powerhouse for the future,

B A C K !

Jim Gentile belonged to a generation of nationally popular Baltimore players who came on board in the late 1950s and early 1960s.

he signed young comers like big Boog Powell, Dean Chance, Bob Saverine, Dave McNally, and Andy Etchebarren.

The O's moved up the ladder a bit in 1959, finishing sixth, and they had fans reeling in the first half of the season as they remained in the first division, roam-ing as high as third. Hoyt Wilhelm won his first nine games. Gene Woodling was the club's leading hitter with a .300 average. Young Brooks Robinson, called up in midseason, hit .284 in eighty-eight games. Bob Nieman hit .292. Durable Milt Pappas posted a 15–9 record with four shutouts.

The Orioles nearly took it all in 1960. Everybody played well. Brooks Robinson was eight for eight in one stretch. He hit .294, was the team's MVP, and began to look like the best third baseman in the league. Jim Gentile drove in ninety-eight runs. Ron Hansen made the All-Star team at shortstop and was voted the league's Rookie of the Year. On the mound, Chuck Estrada won eighteen games, Milt Pappas fifteen, Jack Fisher twelve, Hoyt Wilhelm eleven, and Steve Barber ten. The club registered seven grand slams. The O's sauntered into the first division on May 12 and stayed there the rest of the season. They moved in and out of first place, before wilting in the last two weeks of September and finishing eight games behind the Yankees. Brooks Robinson remembers, "We played very well that year. The Yankee team was one of the best ever, with Mickey Mantle, Roger Maris, and Whitey Ford, and they just pulled away at the end."

MacPhail was certain, absolutely certain, though, that the 1960s would return the Orioles to the glory years.

CHAPTER FIVE

TO THE TOP!
1961–1965

Brooks Robinson smiles warmly when he remembers the Orioles of his youth, the Orioles of the 1960s, one of the best teams ever to play baseball. "In 1960 I looked around at the players, the front office, and the fans, and it was clear to me, right away, that this team was going places."

Of the second season of the decade, he says, "The one word to describe the 1961 season would be 'frustrating.' It was just frustrating. We had a good ball club, a very good ball club, yet we wound up far back." Actually, the 1961 team won ninety-five games, six more than the 1960 team, yet they finished third behind Detroit and the fearsome Yankees. The Yanks were awesome that year, crashing 240 home runs, a new major-league record, with Maris hitting sixty-one and Mantle hitting fifty-four. They won 109 games. Detroit, with Norm Cash hitting a league-leading .361 and Frank Lary winning twenty-three games, was almost as good, winning 101 games.

The O's played well that season. Jim Gentile hit forty-six home runs, drove in 141, and had 314 total bases. He hit five grand slams, including two in consecutive at bats. Dave Philley had twenty-four pinch hits. Brooks Robinson sprayed 163 hits and hit a respectable .287 and improved, again, at third base. The pitching staff had its best year in a

Baltimore fans got the good news of a lifetime when they heard that Frank Robinson, at the peak of his career, had been traded from the Reds to the Orioles.

TO THE TOP!

For Orioles fans, all roads once led to Memorial Stadium.

decade. Steve Barber won eighteen (eight of them were shutouts), Chuck Estrada fifteen, and Milt Pappas thirteen. The mound staff's ERA was 3.22, best in the majors. Yet the O's were third. As Brooks Robinson said, it was frustrating.

Paul Richards, the general manager, left in 1961 to become general manager of the Houston Colt .45s. Lum Harris took his place, but was replaced for the 1962 season by Billy Hitchcock. That season got off to an ominous start when the home opener was scheduled for Friday the thirteenth—it was rained out, however, as was fan appreciation night. As it happened, there wasn't much to appreciate that sea-

TO THE TOP!

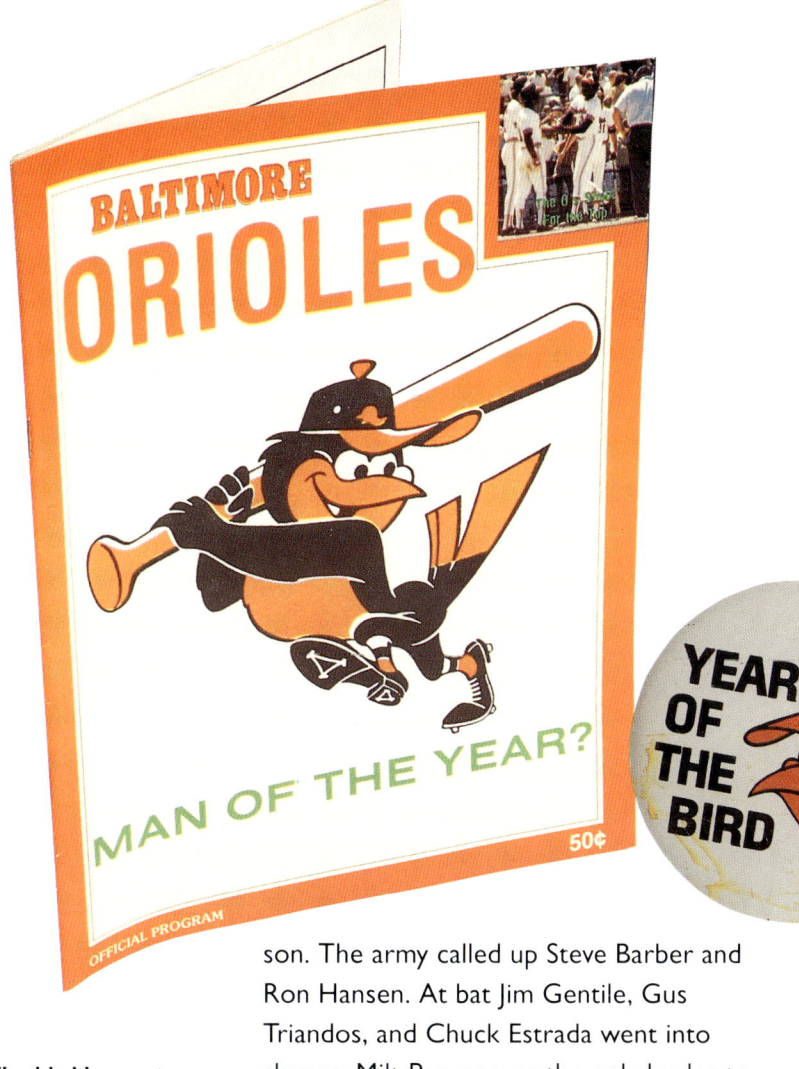

The bird began to wear a scowl in the 1960s, as the Birds got tougher and went after the pennant in earnest.

son. The army called up Steve Barber and Ron Hansen. At bat Jim Gentile, Gus Triandos, and Chuck Estrada went into slumps. Milt Pappas was the only hurler to win more than twelve games. The only bright light was Brooks Robinson, who made the All-Star team and hit a steady .303. By season's end, though, the O's had drowned in seventh place with a stodgy 77–85 record.

Everything turned around in 1963. Maybe it was the stern, no-nonsense scowl that designers put on the Oriole that adorned the team's logo. Maybe it

Brooks Robinson

Brooks Robinson was one of the most unheralded players ever to play in the major leagues. The Orioles were so uncertain of his talents that he spent three years on the bench or in the minors, never playing more than fifty games a season, before he finally started at third base. He was always a problem on the scouting sheets. He wasn't fast. He was weak. He wasn't a power hitter. He never hit for good averages. After meeting him a few times, some even said he was far too nice to develop the "killer instinct" major leaguers needed.

"I just wanted a chance, that's all, and they gave it to me," Robinson says. He made the most of it. In his twenty-three years with the O's (one of the few players to spend a lifetime with one team) Brooks hit .267, with 2,848 hits, 268 home runs, and 1,357 RBIs. In five league championship series he hit .348 and in four World Series he hit .263. He was the league's MVP in 1964 when he hit .317 with 28 homers and 118 RBIs. But it was his fielding that made him legendary. Robinson made fifteen All-Star teams and won

A Brooks bottle cap.

Brooks's home and away jerseys.

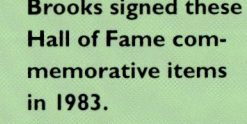

Brooks signed these Hall of Fame commemorative items in 1983.

fifteen Gold Gloves, but his moment of glory was the 1970 World Series. Dubbed "Hoover" after the vacuum cleaner, he made one dazzling play after another against ferocious Cincinnati hitters.

Robinson, now a broadcaster, was elected to the Hall of Fame in 1983. His induction drew one of the largest and most vocal crowds in Hall of Fame history. "I've never seen a group of people with such genuine love of a player," said the hall's associate director, Bill Guilfoile.

And all for a kid who was too slow, too weak, and couldn't hit.

Looking for the typical baseball player for a *Saturday Evening Post* cover, Norman Rockwell chose Brooks.

A Brooks fan collected hundreds of these items in honor of the legendary third baseman.

TO THE TOP!

Steve Barber won twenty games in 1963.

was a rejuvenated Steve Barber, back from the Army. Maybe it was Brooks Robinson's natural leadership, or the big bat of Boog Powell, or the new uniforms. Maybe it was the water in the Chesapeake Bay. Whatever brought about the improvement, the front office liked it. Although the O's didn't seriously contend for the pennant, they were in first place during the first week in June. They finished fourth (the Yankees, naturally, took the pennant with 104 wins), winning eighty-six games and losing seventy-six. Steve Barber won twenty. New relief pitcher Stu Miller, already thirty-five years old, stunned the American League when he appeared in seventy-one games and registered twenty-six saves. He was the Orioles' MVP that year.

Hank Bauer came on as manager in the winter of 1964. The Orioles jumped into the pennant race the first month of the year and by May were near the top. They soon reached first place and remained there for eighty-four long days, at times maintaining a lead of as much as 4½ games. Raw rookie Wally Bunker, who came out of nowhere, won nineteen games (writers starting calling the pitcher's mound Bunker Hill). Brooks Robinson won the MVP award with a sensational season in which he had a .317 average, hit thirty-five doubles, twenty-eight homers, and drove in a

TO THE TOP!

The early 1960s: The *Baltimore Sun* distributed scorebooks with newspapers, all roads seemed to lead to Memorial Stadium, and the Birds were on a roll.

league-leading 118 runs. Milt Pappas had another great year (16–7), and Robin Roberts, a new trade, held his own with a 13–7 record. The O's stayed in the pennant race until the last week of the season, finally slipping to third, just two games out.

Fans were saving all the baseball preview sections in newspapers and magazines in early April 1965. It would be the year, no doubt about it. Common sense dictated that a team that just missed the brass ring by a mere two games was in a good position to grab it on the next try. No such luck, though. The Birds had bad luck all season. The team slumped early. Rain caused ten cancellations that season. A thirty-seven-day newspaper strike eliminated print coverage. There were dozens of promotions, including a planned recreation of the 1945 All-Star game that was never played because of the war, none of which did very well. Fans stayed away. Attendance at one game on a cold September day was just 703.

The last week of the season saw the Orioles win their ninety-fourth and final game, good enough for third place, eight games out. Bauer was disappointed but not demoralized. He and Jerrold Hoffberger, the new owner, knew that the team was better than its finish indicated. After all, despite all the bad luck of 1965, the Orioles had finished only eight games out. The front office was hoping that 1966 would be a better year, that despite tough competition, the O's would push a little harder in 1966 and make it to the top. Then, someone from the front office in Cincinnati called and asked if Baltimore was interested in a trade.

Fans lined up early to buy tickets to Orioles games at Union Park, on Huntingdon Avenue,

CHAPTER SIX

THE GLORY TRAIL
1966–1979

In a move that astonished all of baseball, and Cincinnati fans most of all, the Reds traded Frank Robinson to Baltimore shortly before the 1966 season. Fans made so many protest calls to the Reds switchboard that it literally blew up. The Orioles were startled, too. "When I heard about it, I thought it was a practical joke," remembers Brooks Robinson. "I asked if Sandy Koufax and Willie Mays were part of the deal. Who in their right mind would trade away Frank Robinson?" In a press conference at the time, Reds general manager Bill DeWitt defended the move. "Robinson is not a young thirty. If he were twenty six, we might not have traded him."

Although Cincinnati's Crosley Field had seen all of the great sluggers in baseball history since it was built in 1912, it had never seen the likes of Frank Robinson. Mel Ott smashed home runs over the left-field wall, Willie Mays hit them over the right-field wall, Hack Wilson hit them over both walls, and even Babe Ruth hammered a few out of Crosley. No one, though, hit as many as high and as far as Frank Robinson.

And now he played for the Orioles. The slugger brought the Cincinnati front office to tears from the moment he pulled the Orioles jersey over his wide back. He hit a double in his first at bat in spring training, hit home runs in his first three regular season games, and hit

The peak of O's catcher Ellie Hendricks' career was the 1970 World Series against Cincinnati.

THE GLORY TRAIL

.467 in the first nine. Determined to show Bill DeWitt just what a mistake he had made, and propelled by talent and revenge, Robinson was off to one of the greatest years any athlete in any sport has ever enjoyed.

The Orioles surged into first place in early June, slipping in front of the Yankees. Instead of faltering, as they had done a few times in recent seasons, they surged ahead, beating everybody. No hitter was able to pepper them, and no pitcher was able to ice them. By the end of August the

Frank Robinson needed more hands for all the awards he won in 1966, the year he took the Triple Crown and became the first player ever to be named MVP in both leagues.

Frank Robinson left plenty of bereft Reds fans behind when he was traded to the Orioles, but he was an instant success in Baltimore.

THE GLORY TRAIL

Big Boog Powell, one of the strongest men ever to rock a baseball over a fence, hit 319 homers in his career. Family Night, right, was always a big draw, but most games during the victorious 1966 season drew big crowds.

Birds were in first by ten games and they stayed there as they ran away with the pennant, finishing nine games ahead of Minnesota. Frank Robinson hit .316, with 122 RBIs and forty-nine home runs to win the first Triple Crown in baseball in a decade and the MVP award. The first man to win the MVP in both the American and the National leagues, when named to the All-Star lineup in July, he became the only man to have played in the game for both leagues.

Robinson wasn't the only Oriole who played well that season. Big Boog Powell smashed thirty-four home runs and hit .287. Curt Blefary hit twenty-three homers. Russ Snyder hit .306. The Orioles infield was one of the best in the game: Boog Powell at first, Davey Johnson at second, Luis Aparicio at shortstop, and Brooks Robinson at third.

FRANK ROBINSON

Nearing the end of his career, Frank Robinson hit nineteen home runs for the Dodgers in just over half a season in 1972. Frank was the inspiration for this popular bobbin' head doll.

Frank Robinson arrived with an explosion in 1966. He had played ten years in Cincinnati, averaging thirty-three homers a year and hitting .300-plus, and had taken the MVP in 1961. Dealt to the Orioles in perhaps the most regrettable trade in baseball history (the Reds thought Robinson was too old), the Reds superstar erupted as soon as he arrived in Baltimore, winning the Triple Crown and leading the O's to a pennant and a world championship. His staggering numbers, forty-nine homers, 122 RBIs, and a .317 average, also won him the MVP crown, making him the only man to have won it in both leagues.

He might have won the Triple Crown again in 1967 if not for injuries late in the season. In 1969 he hit .318 with thirty-two homers. In 1970 he hit grand slams in consecutive innings. He was a pitcher's nightmare. "Very, very aggressive, difficult to face," said Gaylord Perry, who pitched against him in both leagues. "He was there to beat you up, to kill you. Maybe the hardest man to get out I ever faced."

Robinson was traded to the Dodgers in 1971 and from there went to the Indians, where he became the first black manager in major-league history. He managed the Giants from 1981 to 1985, twice taking them to the pennant race. He returned to Baltimore as a coach in 1986 and took over as manager when the team struggled at the start of 1988. He took a team that lost 101 games one year and nearly won a pennant with it the next, finishing second by two thin games on the last weekend of the season. He was named manager of the year for his heroics. Robinson later moved up to the front office, where he is a familiar figure around Camden Yards. He often greets fans waving at him. At fifty-nine, he's still not too old.

Robinson put on this jersey when he came to the Orioles in the trade of the century in 1966.

FRANK ROBINSON

He was perhaps the best all-around batter in the majors in his era. He was a very aggressive hitter. He always crowded the plate, challenged you. He'd stand right over the plate and hit a close inside pitch anyway. He would swing at marginal pitches, knowing he could connect. There wasn't a way to get him out, either. Just about everybody has a weak spot. Some guys can't hit down and out curve balls. Some can't hit sliders. Frank could hit everything and he knew that you knew that. It gave him the advantage almost all the time. People say they are amazed that in the 1960s and 1970s he hit 586 home runs. I'm amazed that's all he hit.

—Hall of Fame pitcher Gaylord Perry, who pitched against Robinson in both leagues

Who else but Frank Robinson, with 586 home runs, would adorn this box of cards?

At first Frank Robinson intimidated me. He intimidates lots of people. When he became manager I was actually afraid to talk to him. He had a very commanding presence, and of course next to him every ballplayer in the world looked small. As soon as I got to know him my opinion changed. He's tough, but he's fair and he cares about you and the team. Pretty soon I was friendly with him and his family. He's very helpful to players and he never compares you to him, never tells you how he'd do it.

—Brady Anderson

THE GLORY TRAIL

The *Baltimore Sun* gave away this Orioles scorecard in 1966, the year everyone in town kept their eyes on the Birds as they slugged their way to the World Series.

It wasn't all roses for the Orioles that season. Brooks Robinson fell into the worst slump of his career and hit just .269 that season, though he did manage twenty-three homers. The pitching was lightweight; with just fifteen wins, Jim Palmer was the ace of the staff. If these problems worried manager Hank Bauer, the ex-Marine and former Yankee star, it did not show. He was ready for a world championship and so was all of Baltimore. It would be a tough World Series, too, against a strong Los Angeles Dodgers team led by the dynamic pitching duo of Sandy Koufax and Don Drysdale. That was the year Koufax won twenty-seven games and struck out 317 batters. He was nearly invincible. Not only were the Dodgers going strong in 1966, they were also the defending world champs.

It did not really matter. Frank Robinson hit a two-run homer off Drysdale in the first inning of the first game and Brooks Robinson, up next, slammed a homer, too, setting the tone for the series. Starting pitcher Dave McNally got in trouble in the third inning, but Moe Drabowsky came in to save the 5–2 win. Jim Palmer shut out the Dodgers in game two, 6–0. Back home in Baltimore, Wally Bunker hurled a 1–0 shutout as an overflow crowd roared its approval. The Orioles took game four, 1–0 on a fourth-inning

THE GLORY TRAIL

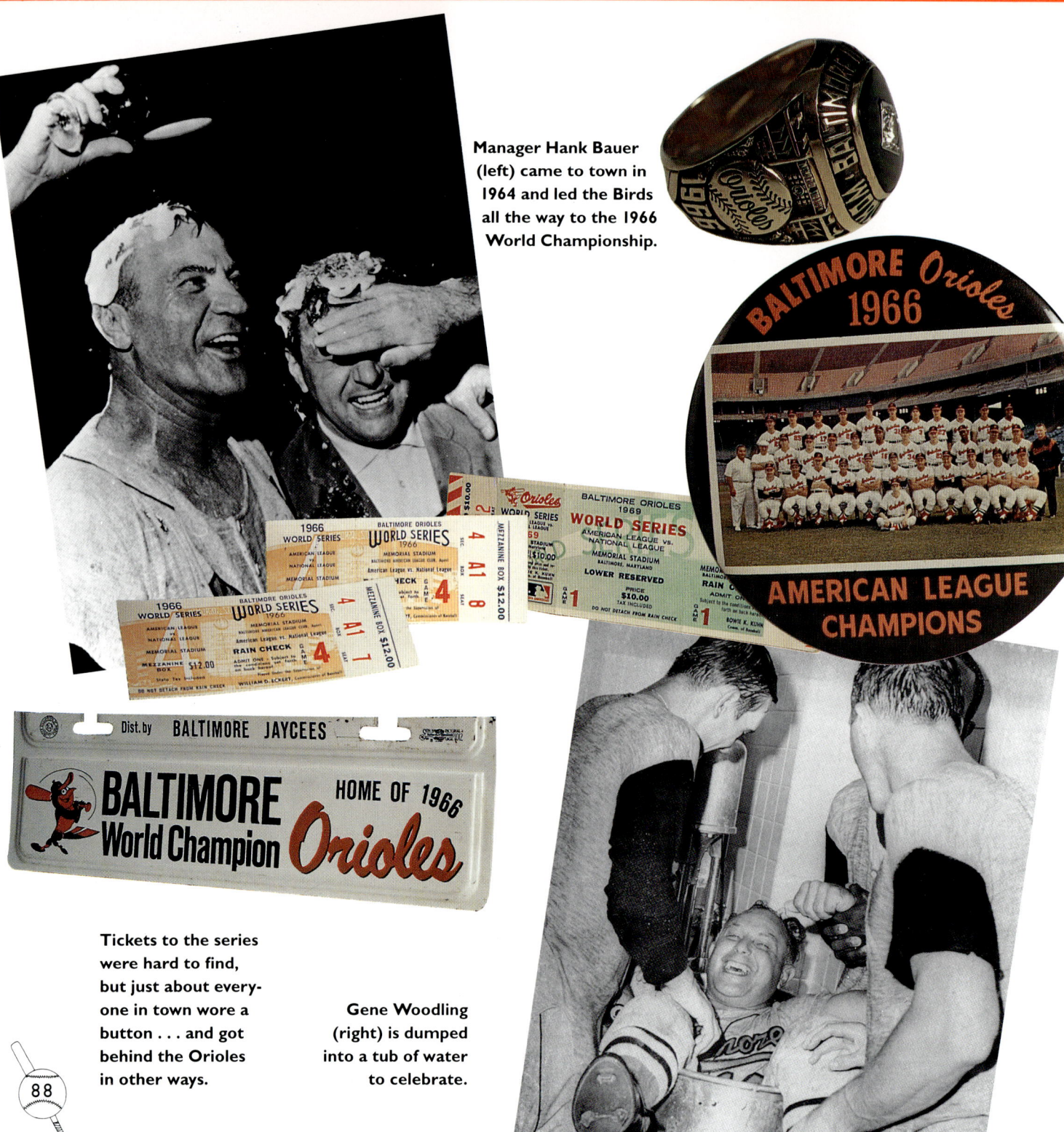

Manager Hank Bauer (left) came to town in 1964 and led the Birds all the way to the 1966 World Championship.

Tickets to the series were hard to find, but just about everyone in town wore a button . . . and got behind the Orioles in other ways.

Gene Woodling (right) is dumped into a tub of water to celebrate.

THE GLORY TRAIL

Earl Weaver, one of the most successful managers in Orioles history, in a familiar scene—being thrown out of a game.

homer by Frank Robinson, capturing the world championship. All told, the Orioles got twenty-four hits and four home runs off the Dodgers, and the O's pitchers, so tentative all season, held the Dodgers to thirty-three consecutive innings without a single run. The screeching headline in the *Baltimore Sun* the next morning said it best: "Orioles Rule Baseball World!"

The 1966 world championship not only gave the O's a crown at last, but it also marked the beginning of a winning era: The team would win pennants in 1969, 1970, 1971, 1979, and 1983; world championships in 1970 and 1983; division titles in 1973 and 1974; and come in second in their division or league eight times over the next twenty-three years.

Some of the punch went out of the Orioles after the 1966 championship, and the Birds stumbled all the way to sixth in 1967. They climbed back up to second in 1968, winning a respectable ninety-one games, but were twelve behind the Tigers, who won 103. Bauer, a popular skipper, was let go in midseason and replaced by Earl Weaver, the first-base coach, who at thirty-seven became the youngest manager in the majors.

The year 1969 was a sad one in Baltimore sports history, as New York proved to be the bane of local teams. Basketball's Bullets lost their chance at the title to the

THE GLORY TRAIL

The Orioles went home with American League championship rings in 1969 . . .

New York Knicks, the Colts lost the Super Bowl to the New York Jets, and the Orioles lost the World Series to the New York Mets. It was a triple tragedy that sports fans are still talking about.

The Orioles were tremendous in 1969. Theirs was maybe the best team in baseball history. They moved into first place quickly, on April 16, and stayed there all year. Earl Weaver quickly became popular with fans (despite feuds with equally popular Jim Palmer from time to time) as he defended his players and berated umpires. Mike Cuellar, an intense screwball pitcher from Cuba, won twenty-three games. Dave McNally won twenty, and Jim Palmer won sixteen. At the plate, Boog Powell socked thirty-seven home runs and hit .304. Mark Belanger hit .287. Brooks Robinson hit only .234, a down year for him, but had twenty-three homers and led the league in assists at third.

Frank Robinson remained torrid, hitting .308, with thirty-two homers and 100 RBIs. Paul Blair, who would have such a long career in Baltimore, hit .285, with twenty-six homers. Don Buford, clutch hitter, hit .291.

After mopping up the American League with 109 wins and clinching the flag by nineteen games, the Orioles shut out a strong Minnesota Twins team in the first-ever divisional playoffs, three games to none. They won the third and final game 11–2, with Paul Blair going five for six, and Don Buford collecting four hits. They moved into the World Series as one of the biggest favorites in baseball history, playing a New York Mets team that had finished next to last the year before. Baltimore fans anticipated another sweep.

It looked like there would be one as of game one, as Don Buford homered off Tom Seaver on his second pitch of the series. Mike Cuellar was near perfect, scattering just six hits, and the O's won

But they lost the series to the New York Mets, four games to one.

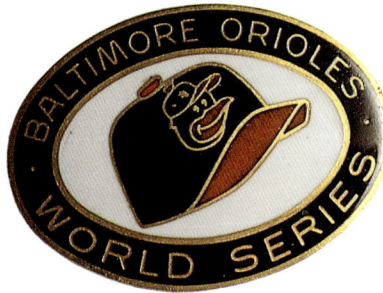

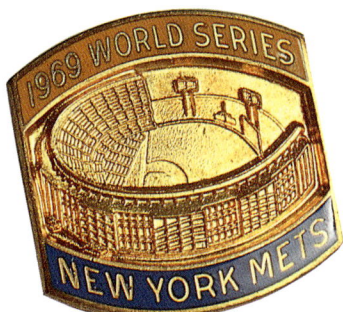

Mike Cuellar pitched for the Havana Sugar Kings in the 1950s, kicked around several major-league U.S. cities, and came to Baltimore in 1969. Over six years he averaged more than twenty wins a season.

You couldn't hit him. You'd swing at him and that was about it. He had a screwball that he could throw at different speeds and take you apart. If you went one for four on him, it was a career day.
—NEW YORK YANKEE ROY WHITE

THE GLORY TRAIL

The O's did it again in 1970, and Baltimore proudly flew souvenir pennants.

"Baseball was close in that series," Mets pitching ace Tom Seaver remembers. "The Orioles were a great team. We were just a little better."

Heads hung low in Baltimore. "We knew we had a good team, and we let it slip away," Brooks Robinson remembers. "I felt I'd let the fans down and that we should have won the thing."

Well, they did win it in 1970. The Birds started just where they left off, moving into first place in April and staying there. They won forty one-run games that season, giving new meaning to the notion of a "cliffhanger." Everybody contributed. Boog Powell did not slow down a bit, crashing thirty-five home runs and hitting .297. Brooks Robinson hit .276, with ninety-four RBIs. Frank Robinson hit .306, with twenty-five homers. Paul Blair hit .267 with eighteen homers. On the mound, the O's were domineering. Dave McNally and Mike Cuellar each won twenty-four games to share the league lead. Jim Palmer won twenty.

In the playoffs, the O's met the Twins again. The Orioles not only swept their opponents, but beat them up, with 10–6, 11–3, and 6–1 wins. Brooks Robinson, who had an average .276 season, sizzled with a .583 average in the playoffs. Powell hit .429. In the World Series the O's met the Cincinnati Reds, Frank Robinson's old

4–1. The Mets, whose fans were calling them the "team of destiny" after their improbable pennant drive, squeaked out a 2–1 win in the ninth inning of game two. The Mets won game three 5–0, and, on a roll now, took game four in the tenth, 2–1, after Ron Swoboda robbed Brooks Robinson of a triple in the ninth. The Mets then won their fourth game in a row, 5–3, and took the series.

"When Swoboda caught that rocket, I knew the fates weren't with us," Boog Powell remembers. "No one else, not even Willie Mays in his finest hour, could have caught that one."

THE GLORY TRAIL

team. The 1970 Reds were the first edition of the fabled Big Red Machine, the team that would dominate the National League for nearly a decade. The lineup already included Tony Perez, Pete Rose, Johnny Bench, and Dave Concepcion.

In game one, the O's were behind 3–0 when big Boog Powell pulled them out of their slump to a 4–3 win. The O's were down again 3–0 for awhile in game two, but Powell hit another home run and Baltimore won it 6–3. In game three, Dave McNally hit a grand slam, and Frank Robinson and Don Buford also homered, for a 9–3 win. The Reds bounced back to win game four, 6–5, but the Orioles took game five and the series, 9–3. All told, the Orioles hit ten homers in the series, but baseball fans are more likely to remember the dazzling way that Brooks Robinson handled third base.

Robinson was a target at third. In a truly great exhibition of talented fielding, he went after twenty-four hits during the series, every one hard and few easy to reach. He jumped to stop some, raced up to scoop others, dove to his right for some and to his left for others. Clips of his brilliant performance are shown again and again as the some of the greatest moments

Brooks Robinson in two of his sensational stops in the 1970 World Series.

THE GLORY TRAIL

in baseball. Looking back, Robinson smiles about his fielding in that series. "In any five games, a third basemen might have four or five balls hit hard at him. In that series the Reds hit everything at me. Sometimes I think they might have been aiming at me."

One of the plays, Robinson admits, amazes him still. He remembers: "There was a curve that hit fair and went into foul territory. I dove right, got it, and turned to throw, off balance, toward first. I think I was almost at the rail when I let it go. I arched it and prayed and I got him by an inch. Every time I see that I say to myself, 'How'd you do that?'"

The victory parade through Baltimore seemed to last longer than the series. The enthusiasm lasted for an entire year, right into the 1971 season, when the O's took their third straight pennant, winning more than a hundred games again. The lineup was as productive as ever (Boog Powell, Frank Robinson, and Brooks Robinson each hit more than twenty homers), but

Paul Blair played for the Orioles for twelve seasons. He hit only .250, but he was a clutch hitter and one of the league's best center fielders.

THE GLORY TRAIL

After the Orioles took the American League championship over Oakland in 1970, bottom, they defeated the Reds in the first game of the World Series.

A glove, recalling Robinson's phenomenal basemanship, dangles from a souvenir 1970s championship pin.

THE GLORY TRAIL

By September 13, 1971, the Orioles had clinched the division, and went on to win the title by twelve games. But they lost the series that year to the Pittsburgh Pirates.

it was the pitching staff that stunned baseball. After long talks with his pitching staff, manager Earl Weaver decided to take a step back in time to the early 1900s, when pitchers threw on four-days' rest, instead of five, and still had twenty- and even thirty-win seasons. Weaver's four starters—Jim Palmer, Mike Cuellar, Dave McNally, and newcomer Pat Dobson—were all for it, and they each won twenty games. (Today, with such big money at stake, the pitchers would not risk a four-day rotation, and the clubs would not allow it, but the formula worked for the Orioles in 1971.)

Once again, the O's swept through the playoffs, this time beating the A's in three straight. They met the Pirates in the series. The O's won the first game on a three-run homer by Merv Rettenmund and solo shots by Frank Robinson and Don Buford. They took game two, 11–3, on fourteen hits (three by Brooks Robinson). The Pirates clawed their way back to win games three, four, and five. The O's halted their slide with a close 3–2 win in game six, with Brooks Robinson's sacrifice fly bringing in the winning run in the tenth inning. The Pirates took the clincher, though, and the world championship, 2–1.

Despite Earl Weaver's brilliant managing, the O's finished third in 1972, but won the Eastern Division title again in 1973 and 1974. In August 1973 the Birds

THE GLORY TRAIL

went on a fourteen-game winning streak, pushing them five games into first. There they stayed, eventually winning ninety-seven games and the division title. In the playoffs the O's met the Oakland A's, the mighty A's of Reggie Jackson, Bert Campaneris, and Gene Tenace. The A's beat the O's, three games to two, and went on to win the World Series.

The 1973 season was a great one for the Orioles, pennant or no pennant. The team hit .266, its highest mark ever. It was the first year of the designated hitter, and the O's Tommy Davis was one of the best, hitting .306. Don Baylor hit .286, and Earl Williams, a newcomer, hit twenty-two homers. Paul Blair hit .280. Earl Weaver was named Manager of the Year that season (umpires didn't vote). On the mound, Mike Cuellar won eighteen games and Dave McNally won seventeen, but the star that summer was Jim Palmer, who won the Cy Young Award with his 22–9 season. Palmer won twenty games in 1973 (he would win twenty or more eight times) on his way to becoming the most successful

This license plate is a little worse for wear, but it is still a reminder of a wonderful era of baseball.

ORIOLE FANS

I took off from work for the first opening day parade in 1954. You never saw a parade like that in your life. There they were, right in front of us, our own *major*-league Orioles, back after fifty-two years. The parade route was lined for miles—six, seven people deep. I don't think anybody in Maryland went to work that day. The players all rode in these big open convertibles and waved and smiled. They tossed hundreds of baseballs into the crowd as they drove by. I remember everybody was so happy. It was like the end of World War II.

—MIKE KAWECKI, OF BALTIMORE

O's caps from various eras.

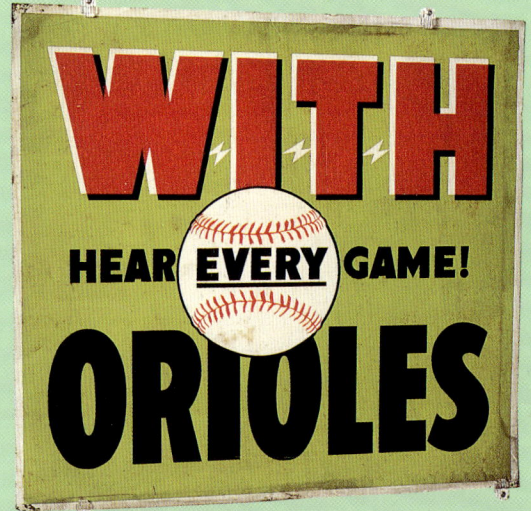

WITH radio brought Orioles baseball to fans all over Maryland.

The Orioles always played good, hard, clean baseball. They always played to win. I like that. They always played as a team. There were superstars, but they never acted like superstars.

—JOE BOSLEY, OF TOWSON

The Senators were Washington's team. The Yankees are New York City's team. What makes the O's special is that their fans come in from all over. They are not just the team of Baltimore. They are all of Maryland's team.

—NANCY SMITH, OF HAGERSTOWN

Or to wear Birds medallions.

Fans are never too young to collect autographs (this one from Boog Powell) or too old to blow on a whistle for a rally . . .

Baltimore has the richest baseball history of any city in America. Cincinnati may have been the birthplace of professional baseball and the Yankees may have won all those World Series, but Baltimore has had teams in the National League, American League, American Association, and International League. No other city had that. And, of course, Baltimore was home to the Baltimore Black Sox and Elite Giants of the Negro Leagues. Our heritage is richer than anyone's.

—GREG SCHWALENBERG, PRESIDENT OF THE BABE RUTH MUSEUM

THE GLORY TRAIL

Jim Palmer hurled his way to the Hall of Fame in this jersey.

I wasn't surprised by the four-man twenty-win season. People always seemed so startled that four of us won twenty games that year. Look at the four. We all had endurance. In 1971, the four of us pitched over one thousand innings. We each had good support from hitters. We were on a good team. We all wanted the ball, wanted to pitch. We all asked for the four-day rotation. We were all in good physical shape. We all had good mental attitudes. Winning twenty for each of us didn't surprise me then and doesn't surprise me now.

—JIM PALMER

THE GLORY TRAIL

In 1970, Dave McNally, Mike Cuellar, and Jim Palmer wound up on the cover of the *Sporting News* when they each won twenty games.

pitcher in the Orioles' long history. Palmer pitched only for Baltimore, winning 268 lifetime and losing just 162. He had a 2.86 ERA, won three Cy Youngs (in 1973, 1975, and 1976), and made six All-Star teams. Gene Michael, general manager of the New York Yankees, remembers Palmer's curve ball. "He had a big, slow curve ball that took half an hour to get to the plate," he says. "When it was working for him, he was practically unhittable." Says former Yankee Mickey Mantle, who faced Palmer for four years, "He'd throw medium speed, nothing you'd be afraid of, and after a few pitches you'd be standing there with the bat on your shoulder and the inning would be over."

In 1974 it was the same broken record again. The O's played brilliantly all year and won the divisional title, yet fell to the streaking A's in the playoffs, this time by three games to one. The A's won the World Series again.

The Orioles fought back in 1975, with Mike Cuellar and Jim Palmer each posting twenty-win seasons, but finished second in the Eastern Division after the Red Sox. The Orioles were frustrated again in 1976, finishing second to the Yankees; in 1977, finishing second to the Yankees again; and in 1978, finishing fourth, nine games out.

This record was not satisfactory to Earl Weaver, who by now had become one

THE GLORY TRAIL

It was easy to smile in 1979, when the Birds took the pennant.

of the most respected managers in the majors and a Baltimore favorite (especially on the day in 1979 when, enraged, he tore a rule book up in front of an umpire). He was named Manager of the Year again in 1979, and he certainly deserved it.

That summer Weaver had only one twenty-or-more game winner, Mike Flanagan (twenty-three) and no .300 hitters. Weaver used every player on his roster and used them often. "I've got depth," he joked. Through some adroit managing, and some power hitting (Eddie Murray, Ken Singleton, and Gary Roenicke all hit more than twenty-five home runs), the O's won the Eastern Division title with 102 victories, then beat the California Angels, three games to one, to take the pennant.

That year the World Series pitted a good Orioles team against a great Pittsburgh team, with Bill Madlock, Willie Stargell, and Dave Parker. It was one of the strangest series in baseball history. Game one, in Baltimore, was rained out, and it snowed the following morning. The temperature had risen to only 41 degrees by the time the game started that afternoon, but the cold didn't chill the Orioles. They won three of the first four games, and it looked certain they would take the series. But, like a Pittsburgh steel worker, the Pirates would not let go. They roared back to bury the Orioles 7–1 in game five,

THE GLORY TRAIL

The 1979 Orioles were the last in a decade of excellent teams, but they lost the series to the powerful Pirates.

then shut them out 4–0 in game six. They took the final game 4–1, becoming one of the few teams ever to be down three games to one and win the series.

For the Orioles, the upset was a heartbreaking end to a decade of excellence during which they finished first or second in their division eight times. In a way it was the final curtain, too. By the end of the 1970s, Frank Robinson and Brooks Robinson were long gone, both retired in 1977, Mike Cuellar, so brilliant earlier in the decade, had been traded. Jim Palmer and Earl Weaver would soon be gone, too. An era was ending.

CHAPTER SEVEN

STREAKING ALONG
1980–1994

The pennant flag of 1979 was raised at Memorial Stadium on Opening Day 1980. Hopes dwindled for another one being raised next to it any time soon as the O's got off to a dreadful start. Nothing went right. The team that just a few years before had won forty one-run games began to lose one-run games. Winning streaks did not last. It wasn't until the middle of June that the Orioles moved above the .500 line, winning as many games as they had lost. With a decent start, they might have beaten the Yankees for the pennant that year. But the Orioles never did catch the Yanks in 1980, and even though they won 100 games, they finished second.

It was a shame, too, because the Orioles played well in 1980. Steve Stone, who arrived in 1979, won the Cy Young Award with a 25–7 record. Scott McGregor won twenty games, and Jim Palmer won sixteen. Eddie Murray, signed to a long-term deal to keep him in Maryland, hit .300. Al Bumbry had 205 hits and hit .318. Ken Singleton hit .304. Attendance jumped a bit in 1980, so Edward Bennett Williams, the Orioles' owner, put an end to talks about the possibility of moving the O's to nearby Washington, D.C.

The 1981 season was a nightmare for baseball as players went on strike on June 12 and shortened the season to 110 games. The strike

The Ripkens in 1987. Cal, Sr., center, was the Oriole manager. Cal, Jr., right, played shortstop, and Billy, left, played second base.

STREAKING ALONG

wreaked havoc with the pennant races because the commissioner's office ruled that whoever was in first place for the first half of the season would play whoever was in first the second half. As a result, the Reds, who had the best record in baseball, didn't even get into the National League playoffs because they didn't finish first in either half. The Orioles didn't get into the American League playoffs because they were two games out in the first half and two games out in the second half. Everybody was frustrated. It was a lost season, but a good one for the 105 games the Birds played (rained out games, which weren't played at a later date under the improvised schedule, robbed them of five of the 110 scheduled games). After a slow start, Eddie Murray hit .294 and led the league with homers, slamming twenty-two. Ken Singleton hit .278. Pitcher Dennis Martinez led the league in wins with fourteen, and Scott McGregor had thirteen (in a full season, both might have won twenty-five).

At the beginning of the 1982 season, a tall (six-feet, four inches), thin kid with long arms and large hands arrived in Baltimore. His name was Calvin Ripken, Jr., and he and friends from Aberdeen, Maryland, a suburb of Baltimore, grew up on Orioles baseball. Ripken soon became another Orioles legend. Ripken hit well that first season—.264, with twenty-eight home runs—but he seemed out of place at third base. Earl Weaver, then in his fifteenth and final year as Orioles skipper, stewed about Ripken and in midseason switched him to shortstop. Critics said if a guy was too tall to play third he was certainly not going to do well at short, where small, wiry men who moved fast always played. Ripken proved Weaver right and went on to become one of the game's great shortstops. Playing in every game, Ripken is on his way to breaking Lou Gehrig's long-standing record of 2,130 consecutive games played.

The O's fielded one of the best teams in years the 1982 season. Eddie Murray hit .316 with thirty-two homers.

A press pass from the strike-shortened 1981 season.

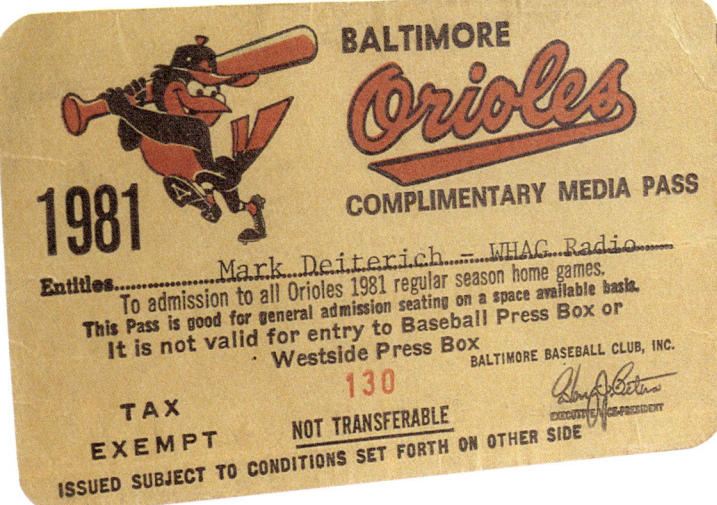

STREAKING ALONG

Cal Ripken's jersey and signature bat.

Ripken's a great ballplayer, with superb skills. He's strong. He has a good eye. He studies pitchers. He keeps in terrific shape. None of that made him great or permitted him to challenge Gehrig's games record. What makes him great is a phenomenal mental toughness. He has incredible concentration and mentally he does not let anything deter him from playing baseball. Everybody gets tired and wants to sit one or two out. Not him. Everybody has family crises and wants to take a few games off. Not him. Everybody is just emotionally beat at times and sits one out. Not him. To get out there every day, month after month, year after year, for thirteen years and never miss a game requires a mental toughness I have never seen in anyone else.

—REGGIE JACKSON

I never wanted to break Lou Gehrig's record. I never wanted to break any record. I just wanted to play baseball every day.

I have a rigid workout program I follow every day, even in the off-season, to stay in shape. When you're in shape you reduce your chances of injury. Suddenly I had five or six years without missing a game. People started to talk about it, and the streak became something of an item. I never thought about it. I only thought about playing each game. It would be heroic to say I once played with a 104 temperature, but I never did. There was luck in it. I've never been really sick; no one in my family was ever very sick.

Now that I'm so close it's all anybody wants to talk about. It's a little annoying, because the writers are missing out on the other players on the team. After the streak ends, I'll keep playing baseball every day. I don't want people to remember me as a guy who played in 2,131 games, but just a guy who wanted to play baseball every day.

—CAL RIPKEN, JR.

Ripken, one of a long line of Orioles superstars, arrived in 1982 and put Baltimore in the sports headlines.

STREAKING ALONG

Baltimore met Philadelphia in the 1983 World Series.

John Lowenstein hit .320 with twenty-four homers. Gary Roenicke hit .270. On the mound, five pitchers won ten or more games. Dennis Martinez had a 16–12 record. Palmer was sensational at 15–5, with eleven in a row. In the end, though, 1982 was a heartbreak year for Ripken and his teammates. On the final day of the season, October 3, the Orioles and the Brewers were deadlocked in first place with one game—against each other—to go. The O's lost it, 10–2. The Brewers went to the playoffs and the Birds went home.

At the end of the season, scrappy manager Earl Weaver, fifty-two, retired his number (4) and moved from the dugout to the broadcast booth. Joe Altobelli replaced him and found one of the best teams in baseball waiting for him in spring training. The Orioles played better than ever in 1983. Eddie Murray had a career year, hitting .306, with thirty-three homers and 111 RBIs. Cal Ripken, never missing a game, was just as good, hitting .318 with twenty-seven homers and 102 RBIs. John Lowenstein hit .281 and Dan Ford hit .280. Jim Palmer, nearing the end of his career, spent time in the minors in rehab with arm trouble, and struggled to a 5–4 mark. Dennis Martinez also had a terrible year, (7–16). Even without these two at full strength, though, the mound staff was brilliant. Scott McGregor won eighteen and Mike Boddicker came up out of the minors to win sixteen, with five shutouts. Storm Davis also came from the minors and had a 13–7 record. Relief pitcher Tippy Martinez saved twenty-one games.

The Orioles took the division by six over Detroit and beat the White Sox, three games to one, for the pennant as Mike Boddicker fanned fourteen in one game and the Birds won in the tenth inning in another. The Orioles faced Philadelphia in the series, which the press promptly dubbed the I-95 series because fans from both cities could make the two-hour drive up or down Interstate 95 to see their teams play. Because the cities were so close, no matter where the game was played the crowd was a heady mix of fans for both teams. No matter what happened in the game, thousands of people would cheer, making for a lively series.

STREAKING ALONG

Companies didn't miss the opportunity to brandish the Orioles, who took their first World Championship in thirteen years in 1983.

STREAKING ALONG

The O's lost the opener, 2–1. In game two, Mike Boddicker, who used the playoffs as a warm up, tossed a three-hitter to even the series. The Birds won game three, 3–2, on two clutch doubles by catcher Rick Dempsey. Game four went to Baltimore, 5–4. Joe Altobelli used four consecutive pinch hitters to get a sixth-inning rally going that gave the O's enough runs to hold off the Phillies in the bottom of the ninth. The fourth win was the easiest. Scott McGregor threw a five-hitter, and Eddie Murray hit two home runs. Rick Dempsey, who was the series MVP for his .385 average and clutch hitting, homered and doubled to clinch the 5–0 win. The Orioles had their first world championship in thirteen years. All of Baltimore celebrated wildly, toasting the Birds in a parade that the city will never forget.

The Orioles were world champs again in 1983.

STREAKING ALONG

Yearbooks, key chains, and other memorabilia celebrate the 1980s Orioles.

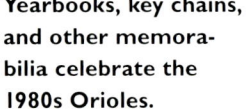

The 1983 series helped lay the cornerstone of a solid fan base. Attendance slipped over the two million mark for the first time in 1983 and climbed steadily through the 1980s to a 2.5 million average. Jim Palmer credits owner Edward Bennett Williams for the jump in attendance. "He realized that baseball had to be marketed like any other business. He promoted us in Washington, D.C., which by the late seventies had lost the Senators, and he promoted us in the suburbs. It paid off."

Lee Sherman, who runs a memorabilia shop in the Baltimore's Inner Harbor, thinks his city simply woke up. "Williams

STREAKING ALONG

The Orioles name emblazoned everything during the winning 1983 season.

was seriously talking about moving the O's out of town, and people realized that they had not only lost football when the Colts moved out of town but might lose the O's and baseball, too."

The 1983 World Series was the last celebration for a few years, though. The O's sagged in 1984, finishing fifth. Eddie Murray again hit over .300 (.306), with twenty-nine homers. Cal Ripken, by then nationally known, hit .304 with twenty-seven homers and led the league shortstops in assists and putouts. Pitcher Mike Boddicker won twenty, and Scott McGregor won fifteen. Jim Palmer retired

In 1984 the modern-day Orioles celebrated their thirtieth anniversary.

STREAKING ALONG

in May, leaving his magnificent Orioles career with a total of 268 wins. Ken Singleton, Al Bumbry, and Benny Ayala left the team in October.

Things did not improve in 1985, and the front office tried everything. Management even brought back Earl Weaver, but he could do little with a team that was in transition. The Orioles won eighty-three and lost seventy-eight that year, though Eddie Murray and Cal Ripken again had fine years.

The 1986 season proved that, like all magicians, Weaver only had so many rabbits in his hat. The O's struggled again, finishing dead last in the division with a 73–89 record. Eddie Murray, as always, was superb, hitting .305. Cal Ripken had yet another fine year, hitting .282 with twenty-five homers. Fred Lynn contributed a .287 average and twenty-three homers. Mike Boddicker won fourteen. It seemed, though, that the Orioles, in the cellar, had no strength left in their wings.

In 1987, the Orioles turned to long-time coach Cal Ripken, Sr., and, keeping

These batting helmets have taken a beating.

STREAKING ALONG

No one will ever fill the shoes of legendary Jim Palmer.

The O's stuck with Cal Ripken, Sr., in 1988, but not for long. After the team opened the season by losing six straight Ripken was canned, and Frank Robinson, who since leaving the O's had distinguished himself as a good manager with bad teams (including the Cleveland Indians), was brought in as skipper. Robinson found himself with a floundering team and could do little, winning just 54 and losing a record 101.

After the O's lost twenty in a row, a joke started going around town: A boy in a custody case said he did not want to live with his father because he beat the boy. He then told the judge he didn't want to live with his mother because she beat him, too.

"Who do you want to live with?" asked the judge.

"The Baltimore Orioles," said the boy. "They don't beat anybody."

Brady Anderson, who joined the O's as an outfielder that summer, remembers, "Frank Robinson was always up, always ready to win," he says. "Ripken played every game like it was the World Series. And the fans were great. No matter how bad we did, they stuck with us. They never let us down."

There were lots of new faces in Memorial Stadium in 1989. Pitcher Bob Milacki was added. Craig Worthington was new at third base, Randy Milligan was at

things in the family, brought Cal Junior's brother, Billy Ripken, up from the minors, to play second. Ripken, Sr., got good performances out of several hitters. He got thirty homers from Eddie Murray, twenty-seven from son Cal, a nice .308 season out of son Billy, twenty-three homers from Fred Lynn, and thirty-one homers from designated hitter Larry Sheets. Ripken didn't get much from the pitching staff, though, and the Oriole hitting power was never quite enough to win ball games. Mike Boddicker won just ten games and was the ace of the staff.

STREAKING ALONG

Frank Robinson left Baltimore as a player in 1972, but came back as a manager in 1988.

first. Mike Devereaux was brought up from the minors to play center field, Phil Bradley played left. Bob Melvin was the new catcher. Eddie Murray was gone, traded to the Dodgers. Fred Lynn and Mike Boddicker were gone.

The Orioles did not play spectacular baseball in 1989, but with Robinson pushing and nudging them, they kept winning. The O's kept pace with Toronto, New York, and Milwaukee through the first half of the season, and stayed with Toronto through the second half. They were always close. It wasn't a great year for any of the Birds. Cal Ripken was the only man to hit twenty homers. Joe Orsulak's .285 was the highest average on the team. No pitcher won twenty. Ballard's 18–8 was the best record. But the Orioles did win. They won by one run, two runs. Toronto did not play great ball, either. As the two teams went into the final week of the season they were neck and neck. Finally, Toronto edged out Baltimore by two games.

The Orioles of the 1990s have a distinctly different look. The front office keeps the best of the veterans, experiments with the new, and builds a strong farm system. They produce contenders each year. Record crowds now fill the Orioles new, harborside ballpark, Camden Yards (attendance was an astonishing 3.5 million in 1992, the opening year)

Camden Yards

The view from the upper deck shows Camden Yards' location in the heart of the city; a pennant from the first game in the park is a collector's item.

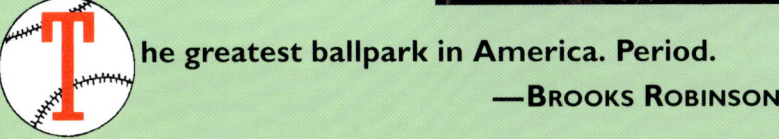

The greatest ballpark in America. Period.
—Brooks Robinson

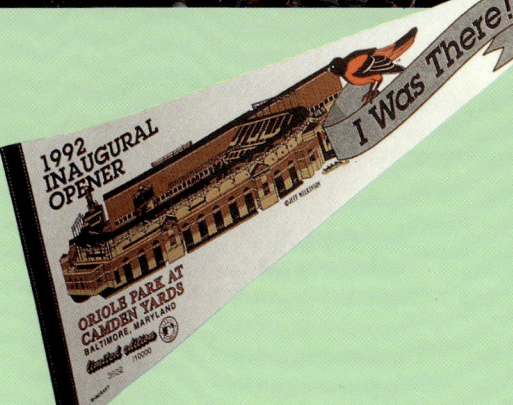

Camden Yards

Eutaw Street, closed to traffic, runs alongside the stadium and is lined with shops and restaurants. The O's executive offices occupy an old brick warehouse.

Everything about the Yards, right down to the suspenders and shirts of the ushers, is a throwback to the good old days.

America's collective memory inspired Camden Yards, the 48,041-seat, $105 million ballpark that was built very new to look very old. The old B & O warehouse behind right field (exactly 426 feet from home plate) lends the park the look of a ballfield set in the middle of an old urban neighborhood. The center-field wall has ivy growing up it, much like the wall at Chicago's Wrigley Field. There is a groundskeeper's shed built into the right center-field wall, just as there was a shed in left field at old Oriole Park. The ballplayer logo built into the aisle seats is reminiscent of the "NY" on the old Polo Grounds chairs.

An old-fashioned clock crowns the high-tech scoreboard.

A bird motif adds decorative touches throughout the Yards.

While the park may look old, it feels brand new. Camden Yards is a hi-tech, state-of-the-art facility built for the comfort of the fans. There are picnic areas beyond the center-field fence and a porch for bystanders to watch the game over the right-field wall. Eutaw Street, running alongside the park, is lined with modern, open-air barbecue pits, peanut stands, souvenir shops, and restaurants in the ground floor of the B & O warehouse.

The park, so popular with fans that the biggest-selling tee-shirts are not of the players but the ballpark, has become a tourist attraction. A check of hotel records shows that 12 percent of the people in the stadium every night are from at least 120 miles away and sleep over somewhere in town. Many fans drive four hours from New York or New Jersey to the ballpark, see the game, and drive four hours home. The Yards is so popular that more than fifteen thousand people take one of the seven daily tours of the stadium each year. Nearly all games are

Camden Yards

sold out. Thousands stop by before games to dine on Eutaw Street.

A throwback to the great ballparks in history, the Yards has become so popular that nearly a dozen major- and minor-league ballparks with that same new-to-look-old architectural style are under construction or have recently opened, such as the new Durham Bulls Stadium, in North Carolina.

The purists still argue that it just looks new, that it's manufactured nostalgia, too pretty to be realistic. Nobody at the stadium cares much about that. They're too busy watching the ball game and ducking behind the center-field wall when they see that 1892 sign that warns "Watch out for Batted Balls."

The oversize Birds mascot takes a rest in its new pen.

 We drive four hours down, see the game, sleep over, and drive four hours back. It's worth it. This ballpark is a national treasure.
—JOHN AGULIAN, OF MORGANVILLE, NEW YORK

The Yards is a state of the art Fenway, a Wrigley with comfort.
—STEVE AUSTIN, OF BALTIMORE

A typical game-day scene at the Yards, and Cal Ripken, Jr., at bat in his new home.

Camden Yards throws you back in time, to when you were a kid and saw baseball in parks like this. It's like they brought this back out of the mist, retrieved it from your best memories.
—DAVID SEGUI

STREAKING ALONG

A glittering display commemorates the Birds' many championships.

STREAKING ALONG

Old Memorial Stadium is no longer home, but it is not forgotten.

The American League put the 1993 All-Star game in the major-league's newest stadium.

to cheer such new players as Leo Gomez, David Segui, Jeffrey Hammonds, and Jack Voigt.

The struggling O's were fifth in 1990 and sixth in 1991. With huge crowds cheering for them every night at the new Camden Yards, the Birds surged into third place in 1992. The O's had a good year in 1993, finishing third in the American League East and enjoying some long winning streaks.

Just a long fly ball from Camden Yards, at Pratt and Emory streets, is a narrow, brick row house where Babe Ruth was born, now the Babe Ruth Museum. Curator Greg Schwalenberg has collected an archive of old Orioles' photos. All of the Orioles from the great teams of the 1890s look down from a wall facing Camden Yards. They are all smiling.

ORIOLES GREATS

LEFTY GROVE

This superb left-hander was probably the best pitcher in America during the 1920s. Grove, who became known as "Groves" early in his career when he mistakenly signed his name with an "s," played with Baltimore and the Philadelphia A's, but since Baltimore was a minor-league club in the International League his stunning seasons there received little national recognition. Grove arrived in Baltimore as an eighteen-year-old flamethrower in 1918. He quickly became one of the top pitchers in the league, winning 108 games and losing only 36 in seven seasons. He was the league's strikeout king, fanning 1,118 in just four seasons and an incredible 330 in 1923 alone. Grove repeatedly pleaded with manager Jack Dunn to let him move to the majors, but Dunn refused, keeping the pitcher until 1925, when he couldn't turn down an offer of $100,000 for him from the A's.

Grove, a hurler with a bad temper, did not slow down with Philadelphia. He led the American League in strikeouts for seven consecutive years, went on to win three hundred games, and made the Hall of Fame. Baseball purists insist that if Grove had gone to the majors when he should have, in 1919 or 1920, he would have won more than four hundred games.

WEE WILLIE KEELER

A slight outfielder, just five feet four inches tall, "Wee Willie" was a giant of a hitter. Unlike the sluggers to come, Keeler was a scientific batter whose goal was simply to get on base, not to batter the outfield walls. He moved his hands up and down the bat in order to rap hits between infielders or just over their heads, or to smash

the ball into the ground and make it bounce high in the air while he raced to first base (a technique that came to be called the "Baltimore chop").

Asked what the secret to his .345 lifetime average was, he replied, "Hit 'em where they ain't." He did. Keeler grew into a legend in Baltimore. He hit .361 in his first full season there and then tore up the National League with consecutive season averages of .391, .386, .424, and .385. Keeler later played four seasons with the Brooklyn Dodgers and eight with the New York Yankees, but he gained his fame in Baltimore.

WILLIE KEELER

JOHN McGRAW

John McGraw

"Muggsy" McGraw, the cantankerous player-manager, first arrived in Baltimore as a player in the old American Association franchise in 1891, then moved to the new Orioles franchise in 1892. A fine hitter, he averaged .344 in his nine seasons with Baltimore. He gained even more notoriety as a pit bull of a base runner, knocking over infielders while running, and sliding and blocking runners himself as a third baseman.

An obstinate ballplayer, McGraw refused to be traded to Brooklyn by Hanlon, who owned an interest in both clubs, because he and Wilbert Robinson owned a bar in Baltimore. He became manager of the O's in 1899, went to Saint Louis (in the National League) as manager in 1900, and then came back to Baltimore in 1901 with the American League franchise. He left again in 1902 after spats with league officials and moved to New York, where his teams finished first or second in twenty-one of twenty-nine seasons, taking ten pennants and three world championships.

ORIOLES GREATS

Jim Palmer

This high-kicking pitcher was a fictional Frank Merriwell come-to-life in the glory years of the 1960s. He signed on in 1963, an untried seventeen-year-old kid, and worked his way into the rotation at age twenty in 1966, when, with one of the Birds' wonder teams, he won fifteen and became the youngest man to win a complete World Series game. A brilliant career almost ended with arm trouble that sent Palmer down to the minors for parts of two seasons. Successful surgery restored his arm in time for the 1969 season, when he went 16–4, and 1970, when he posted the first of his eight twenty-win seasons (he is one of only three American League pitchers with that many). Palmer went on to win 268 games, becoming the winningest pitcher in Baltimore history, take three Cy Young Awards, and pitch in six All-Star games.

Palmer was a workhorse and a money pitcher. He won the pennant clinchers for the O's in 1966, 1969, 1970, and 1971, and established league championship series records for strikeouts and complete games. He pitched brilliantly into the 1980s and in 1983 became the first pitcher in history to win World Series games in three decades. The popular Palmer later gained fame posing for underwear advertisements and as a broadcaster.

Milt Pappas

Milt Pappas came up as a raw rookie at age nineteen in 1958, after just three minor-league starts, and won ten games. He went on to be one of the steadiest pitchers in baseball, winning 209 games for the O's, Reds, and Cubs without ever winning more than seventeen in a single season.

Pappas was a productive pitcher for the O's, winning an average of fifteen games a year in his eight summers there. A chronic whiner in his early years, Pappas left Baltimore suddenly in a 1966

ORIOLES GREATS

trade when the O's had a chance to land Frank Robinson from the Reds. Pappas was mediocre for the Reds, but did finish his career with two fine years for the Cubs in 1971 and 1972.

CAL RIPKEN, JR.

Baltimore's steady shortstop, Cal Ripken, Jr., should soon make baseball history when he breaks the immortal Lou Gehrig's 56-year-old record of 2,130 consecutive games played. That would be glory enough for any man, but it is just one of the many trophies on the Iron Man's shelf. Ripken, whose father managed and coached the O's and whose brother played second base for them, joined the team in 1982, a lackluster third baseman with a weak bat. Earl Weaver, sensing he had a round peg in a square hole, moved him to shortstop in midseason and the towering infielder (at six feet four inches, he is the tallest shortstop in the game) bloomed, hitting twenty-eight homers and winning rookie of the year honors.

He was even better in his sophomore season, hitting .318 and winning MVP honors. A born slugger with power in his big frame, he smashed twenty homers eight years in a row, breaking Ernie Banks's homer record for shortstops. Ripken continued to hit well and build on his consecutive game streak through the 1980s, but surprisingly slowed down in 1987, hitting just .252. More lackluster seasons followed in 1988, 1989, and 1990, and some fans thought Ripken was finished. Then in a burst of brilliance, Ripken jolted all of baseball with a sterling 1991 season. He hit .326, with 34 homers, and won the MVP title (he was also MVP of the All-Star game). He was back.

ORIOLES GREATS

Brooks Robinson

As long as baseball is played, Brooks Robinson will be remembered for his dramatic fielding in the 1970 World Series. A one-man vacuum cleaner, he played brilliantly, helping bring Baltimore the world title that October. Brooks was one of the greatest fielders of all time, winning Gold Gloves at third base in sixteen of his twenty-three seasons and making the All-Star team fifteen times.

Robinson's glove often overshadowed his hitting, which was prodigious. Although he never made particularly high averages (he hit .268 lifetime), he had 1,357 RBIs and 268 home runs. Robinson, one of the most generous and popular ballplayers ever, later became a successful broadcaster.

Frank Robinson

In 1966 the Orioles became the proud recipients of the worst trade in the history of baseball. Thinking Frank Robinson had peaked after his 1965 season (.296 batting average, 33 home runs), the Reds traded him to the O's. Robinson, still in great shape and angry about the trade, proceeded to win the Triple Crown (.316 average, 49 homers, 122 RBIs) and the Most Valuable Player title (the only man to ever win MVP in both leagues), and led the Birds to the World Championship. Proving it was no fluke, the slugger went on to hit 179 homers, drive in 550 runs, and hit .300 in six seasons with Baltimore. He might have won the Triple Crown again in 1967, but late-season injuries prevented him.

Robinson became baseball's first black manager in 1974, when he was named skipper of the Cleveland Indians. After moderately

ORIOLES GREATS

successful stints with the Indians, Angels, and Giants, he returned to the Orioles as a coach in 1986 and in 1988 became manager. In 1989 his Birds were in first place at the All-Star break, but lost the pennant on the final weekend of the year. Robinson was named manager of the year. He later moved to the front office.

Earl Weaver

Manager Earl Weaver never played in the major leagues and spent ten years managing in the minors before he moved up to the Orioles. Weaver debuted with a bang, though, winning the pennant in his second season with the O's, 1969, and taking the World Championship in 1970 and pennants in 1971 and 1979. In a game in which some teams will have ten managers in ten years, Weaver was the O's only skipper for fifteen straight seasons, 1968 to 1982, and came back for two seasons in 1985 and 1986 before retiring.

Weaver was a controversial figure. He carried on well-publicized feuds with umpires and was tossed out of nearly one hundred games (one day in 1985 he was even thrown out of both games of a doubleheader) and suspended four different times. He feuded with some players, including pitcher Jim Palmer, and was often the target of critical fans (particularly in 1969 when his powerful team was upset in the World Series by the Miracle Mets). On retirement, though, his scorecard showed a world title, four pennants, and appearances in six league championship series.

ORIOLES STATS

ORIOLES ALL-TIME PITCHING LEADERS

EARNED RUN AVERAGE (500 OR MORE INNINGS)
S. Miller	2.37
Wilhelm	2.42
Watt	2.73
Dobson	2.78
Palmer	2.86
O'Dell	2.86
Hall	2.89
Hardin	2.95
Phoebus	3.06
Roberts	3.09

STRIKEOUTS
Palmer	2,212
McNally	1,476
Flanagan	1,297
Cuellar	1,011
Pappas	944
Barber	918
McGregor	904
D. Martinez	858
Boddicker	836
T. Martinez	584

GAMES
Palmer	558
T. Martinez	499
Flanagan	450
McNally	424
Watt	363
McGregor	356
Hall	342
D. Martinez	319
Stewart	307
S. Miller	297

WINS
Palmer	268
McNally	181
Cuellar	143
Flanagan	141
McGregor	138
Pappas	110
D. Martinez	108
Barber	95
Boddicker	79
Hall	65

INNINGS
Palmer	3,947.2
McNally	2,653.0
Flanagan	2,317.2
McGregor	2,141.1
Cuellar	2,028.0
D. Martinez	1,775.1
Pappas	1,632.0
Barber	1,415.0
Boddicker	1,273.2
H. Brown	1,032.0

SHUTOUTS
Palmer	53
McNally	33
Cuellar	30
Pappas	26
McGregor	23
Barber	19
Flanagan	17
Boddicker	13
Phoebus	11
D. Martinez	10

LOSSES
Palmer	152
Flanagan	116
McNally	113
McGregor	108
D. Martinez	93
Cuellar	88
Barber	75
Pappas	74
Boddicker	73
Ballard	51

SAVES
Olson	131
T. Martinez	105
S. Miller	92
Watt	72
Stoddard	57
Hall	51
Aase	50
Stanhouse	45
Stewart	42
Wilhelm	40

WON-LOST PCT (MINIMUM 50 DECISIONS)
Stone	.656 (40–21)
Palmer	.638 (268–152)
Bunker	.620 (44–27)
Cuellar	.619 (143–88)
Hall	.619 (65–40)
McNally	.616 (181–113)
Pappas	.598 (110–74)
Davis	.586 (61–43)
Dobson	.581 (36–26)
Hardin	.576 (36–28)

ORIOLES ALL-TIME BATTING LEADERS

GAMES
B. Robinson	2,986
Belanger	1,962
Murray	1,820
C. Ripken	1,800
Powell	1,763
Blair	1,700
Singleton	1,446
Bumbry	1,428
Dempsey	1,245
Dauer	1,140

RUNS
B. Robinson	1,232
Murray	1,048
C. Ripken	1,043
Powell	796
Bumbry	772
Blair	737
Singleton	684
Belanger	670
F. Robinson	555
Dauer	448

HOME RUNS
Murray	333
Powell	303
C. Ripken	273
B. Robinson	268
Singleton	182
F. Robinson	179
Triandos	142
Blair	126
Gentile	124
L. May	123

BATTING AVERAGE (MINIMUM 1,200 AT BATS)
Nieman	.303
Boyd	.301
F. Robinson	.300
Murray	.295
T. Davis	.291
Rettenmund	.284
Singleton	.284
Bumbry	.283
Orsulak	.281
Lacy	.280

AT BATS
B. Robinson	10,654
C. Ripken	6,942
Murray	6,845
Powell	5,912
Belanger	5,734
Blair	5,606
Singleton	5,115
Bumbry	4,958
Dauer	3,829
Dempsey	3,585

HITS
B. Robinson	2,848
Murray	2,021
C. Ripken	1,922
Powell	1,574
Singleton	1,455
Blair	1,426
Bumbry	1,403
Belanger	1,304
Dauer	984
D. Johnson	904

TOTAL BASES
B. Robinson	4,270
Murray	3,421
C. Ripken	3,178
Powell	2,748
Singleton	2,274
Blair	2,175
Bumbry	1,883
Belanger	1,604
F. Robinson	1,598
Triandos	1,351

STOLEN BASES
Bumbry	252
Blair	167
Aparicio	166
Belanger	166
Baylor	118
Anderson	102
Buford	85
Grich	77
Wiggins	71
Murray	61

TRIPLES
B. Robinson	68
Bumbry	52
Blair	51
Aparicio	34
C. Ripken	34
Belanger	33
Grich	27
Devereaux	25
Murray	25
Brandt	22

RUNS BATTED IN
B. Robinson	1,357
Murray	1,190
Powell	1,063
C. Ripken	1,014
Singleton	767
Blair	567
F. Robinson	545
Triandos	517
L. May	487
Gentile	398

AUTOGRAPH PAGE

BIBLIOGRAPHY

Alexander, Charles. *John McGraw.* New York: Penguin, 1988.

Beard, Gordon. *Birds on the Wing: The Story of the Baltimore Orioles.* Garden City, N.J.: Doubleday, 1967.

Bready, James. *The Home Team.* Baltimore, Md.: 1984.

Durso, Joseph. *The Days of Mr. McGraw.* Englewood Cliffs, N.J.: Prentice-Hall, 1969.

Holway, John. *Blackball Stars.* Westport, Conn.: Meckler Books, 1988.

Lieb, Frederick. *The Baltimore Orioles.* New York: G. P. Putnam's Sons, 1955.

Petersen, Robert. *Only the Ball Was White.* Englewood Cliffs, N.J.: Prentice-Hall, 1970.

Pluto, Terry. *The Earl of Baltimore: The Story of Earl Weaver.* Piscataway, N.J.: New Century Press, 1982.

Robinson, Brooks, and Fred Bauer. *Putting It All Together.* New York: Hawthorn Books, 1971.

Shatzkin, Mike. *The Ballplayers.* New York: William Morrow, 1990.

Wolff, Rick, ed. *The Encyclopedia of Baseball.* New York: Macmillan, 1990.

INDEX

(Page numbers in *italic* refer to illustrations.)

A
brams, Cal, 64, 65
advertisements, *17, 22, 29, 58, 59*; on scorecards, *24, 32*
Agulian, John, 121
alarm clock, *65*
All-Star games, 67, 71, 75, 76, 79, 83, 101; of 1958, 68–69, *69*; of 1993, *123*
all-time batting leaders, 131
all-time pitching leaders, 130
Altobelli, Joe, 109, 111
American Association, 16–17, 19, 32–33, 49
American League, 11, 21, 32–36, 43, 44, 45, 47, 49, 59, 69, 83
Anderson, Brady, 86, 115
Aparicio, Luis, 83
Arlett, Buzz, 53
Atlantic Association, 19
attendance figures, 31, 63–65, 66, 68, 79, 112–13, 116
Austin, Steve, 121
autographs, *99*, 113; on baseballs, *12*, 76
Ayala, Benny, 114

B
aker, Home Run, 43
Baltimore Base Ball Club, *14, 16*
Baltimore Black Sox, 38
"Baltimore chop," 21
Baltimore Elite Giants, 38–39, *39*
Baltimore Lord Baltimores, 15–16, 38
Baltimore Orioles: from 1855 to 1898, 15–29; from 1899 to 1916, 31–45; from 1919 to 1953, 47–59; from 1954 to 1960, 61–71; from 1961 to 1965, 73–79; from 1966 to 1979, 81–103; from 1980 to 1994, 105–23; fans of, 98–99, 115; great players of, 124–29; stats for, 130–31; thirtieth anniversary of, *113*. See also specific players, managers, and topics
Baltimore Premier Athletic Club, 35
Baltimore Sun, 87, *87*
Baltimore Terps, 43–44, 45, 47
Barber, Steve, 71, 74, 75, *78, 78*
Barnie, Billy, 18, 19
baseball cards, *37*; "cabinet" cards, *16*; with F. Robinson on box, *86*
baseballs: autographed, *12*, 76; commemorating B. Robinson, *77*
batboy: uniform of, *10*
bats: of Maisel, 44; of Ripken, *107*; of B. Robinson, 76; of Ruth, *42*; wide-handled, *34*
batting helmets, 114
Bauer, Hank, *12*, 78, 79, 87, *88*, 89
Baylor, Don, 97
beer ads, *17, 24, 58, 59*
Belanger, Mark, 13, 90
Bench, Johnny, 93
Bentley, Jack, *12*, 49, 50
Biot, Charles, 39
bird motifs, 70, *75*, 119
Bishop, Max, 49, 50
Black, Joe, 38, 39
black baseball, 38–39
Blair, Paul, 13, 90, 92, 94, 97
Blefary, Curt, 83
bobbin' head doll, *84*
Boddicker, Mike, 109, 111, 113–16
Boley, Joe, 49
books and booklets: by Dunn, *41*; scorebooks, *22, 67, 70, 79*; "sketchbooks," *21*
Bosley, Joe, 98
Boston Braves, 18, 58
Boston Red Sox, 44, 45, 101
bottle cap, *76*
bottles: Coke, *113*
Boyd, Bob, 68
Bradley, Phil, 116
Bresnahan, Roger, 33, 35

Brooklyn Dodgers, 29, 31, 37, 38, 39, 44
Brouthers, Dan, *12*, 20, 21, 27, *28*
Browning, Pete, 23
Buford, Don, 90, 93, 96
Bugle Field, *13*, 39
Bumbry, Al, 105, 114
Bunker, Wally, 78, 87
Burns, Oyster, 18
buttons, *87*

C
abinet" cards, *16*
calendar, *42*
California Angels, 102
Camden Yards, 11, 13, 116, *117–21*, 118–21
Campanella, Roy, 38, *38*–39
Campaneris, Bert, 97
caps, *98*; of Palmer, *13*
Cash, Norm, 73
championship rings, 56, 87, 90, 96, 111, *122*
Chance, Dean, 71
Chicago White Sox, 21, 63, 65, 109
Cincinnati Reds, 79, 81–82, 84, 92–94, 106
Civil War, 11, 15
Clarke, Boileryard, 61
Cleveland Indians, 85, 115
clock, *65*
Cobb, Ty, 28
Coke bottles, *113*
Collins, Eddie, 43
Colored World Series, 38, 39
Concepcion, Dave, 93
Courtney, Clint, 63
Cree, Birdie, 45
Cuellar, Mike, 13, 90, *91*, 92, 96, 97, 101, *101*, 103
cups, 77
Cy Young Award, 97, 101, 105

D
anforth, Daring Dave, 41
Davis, Storm, 109
Davis, Tommy, 97

Dempsey, Rick, 111
Detroit Tigers, 28, 36–37, 73, 89, 109
Devereaux, Mike, 116
DeWitt, Bill, 81, 82
dinners: honoring Orioles, *56*
Dobson, Pat, 96
Donlin, Mike, 33
Doolan, Mickey, 44
Doyle, Jack, 61
Drabowsky, Moe, 87
draft rule, 48
Drysdale, Don, 87
Dunn, Jack, 11, 33, *34*, 37, 37–45, *40, 41*, 47–50
Dunn, Jack, III, 53
Dygert, Jimmy, 41

E
arnshaw, George, *12*, 49
Eastern Colored League, 38
Egan, Ben, 49
Estrada, Chuck, 71, 74, 75
Etchebarren, Andy, 71

F
amily Night: scorecard for, *83*
fans, 98–99, 115; attendance figures and, 31, 63–65, 66, 68, 79, 112–13, 116
Federal League, 43–44, 47
Federal League Park (later Oriole Park), 43, 47, 53, 55
Field Day: program for, *25*
Fisher, Jack, 71
Flanagan, Mike, 102
flyers, *62*
Ford, Dan, 109
Ford, Whitey, 71
Fornieles, Mike, 67
Frank, Sidney, 33

G
ardner, Billy, 68
Gastall, Tom, 68
Gehrig, Lou, 13, 106, 108
Gentile, Jim, 71, *71*, 73, 75
Gilliam, Junior, 38
Gleason, Kid, *12*, 21

134

gloves: of Palmer, *13;* of Ruth, 42
Gold Gloves, 77
Goldman, Harry, 33
Gorman, Arthur, 15
Grier, Red, 38
Griffith, Clark, 61
Grove, Lefty, 12, 50, *51,* 124
Guilfoile, Bill, 77

Hall of Fame, 21, 23, 27, 77; commemorative items from, 76
Hanlon, Ned, 11, 19–23, 24, 28, 31, 36, 37, 40
Hansen, Ron, 71, 75
Harridge, Will, 61
Harris, Lum, 74
Hauser, Joe, 53
helmets, *114*
Hendricks, Ellie, *80*
Heydler, John, 27
Hitchcock, Billy, 74
Hoffberger, Jerrold, 79
Holmes, Oliver Wendell, 45
Honig, John, 49
Houston Colt .45s, 74

International League, 12, 36, 41, 47, 49, 53, 54

Jacket: of Barber, *78*
Jackson, Reggie, 97, 107
Jennings, Hughie, 12, *19,* 20, 21, 23, 28, 31, 36, 36–37
jerseys: of Palmer, *100;* of Ripken, *107;* of B. Robinson, *76;* of F. Robinson, *85*
Johnson, Ban, 32–35
Johnson, Connie, 67
Johnson, Davey, 83
Junior World Series, 49, 53, 54–57

Kawecki, Mike, 98
Keeler, Wee Willie, 12, 20, 21, 27–28, 31, 124–25
Kell, George, 67
Kelley, Joe, 20, 21, 29, 31, 35
Kennedy, Bob, 65
key chains, *112*
Kilroy, Matt, 11, 18, *18*
Knabe, Otto, 44
Koufax, Sandy, 87

Landis, Kenesaw Mountain, *40*
Lary, Frank, 73
Lawrey, Otis, 49
League of Colored Baseball Clubs, 38
license plate, *97*
Los Angeles Dodgers, 85, 87–89, 116
Louisville Colonels, 20, 28, 54–57
Lowenstein, John, 109
Lynn, Fred, 114, 115, 116

McGinnity, Joe "Iron Man," 33, 35
McGraw, John, 11, 12, 20, *20,* 21, 23, 27, *27,* 28–29, 31–35, *33, 40,* 43, 65, 125
McGraw, Mrs. John, 61
McGregor, Scott, 105, 106, 109, 111, 113
Mack, Connie, 41, 61
McMahon, Sadie, 20, 21
McNally, Dave, 13, 71, 87, 90, 92, 93, 96, 97, *101*
MacPhail, Lee, 70–71
Madlock, Bill, 102
Maisel, Fritz, 41, 44, 49, *49*
Maisel, George, 41
Mantle, Mickey, 71, 73, 101
Maris, Roger, 71, 73
Martinez, Dennis, 106, 109
Martinez, Tippy, 109
Maryland Baseball Park, 38

mascots, *120;* uniform of, *10*
Mays, Willie, 81, 92
medallions, 99
Melvin, Bob, 116
Memorial Stadium, 13, 63, 64, 74, *123;* sign for, *79*
Meyer, Benny, 44
Michael, Gene, 101
Milacki, Bob, 115
Miles, Clarence, 59
Miller, Stu, 78
Milligan, Randy, 115–16
Milwaukee Brewers, 109
Minnesota Twins, 90, 92
Moore, Ray, 67
Municipal Stadium, 54, 58
Murphy, Eddie, 41
Murray, Eddie, 102, 105, 106, 109, 111, 113–16

National Association of Base Ball Players, 15
National Association of Professional Baseball Players, 11, 15
National League, 11, 16–17, 19, 23, 28, 43, 44, 45, 47, 65, 83, 93
Negro National League, 38
Newark Peps, 43
newspaper clippings, *13, 55, 95*
Newton Park, 38
New York Giants, 21, 29, 35, 40, 43, 49
New York Mets, 90, 90–92
New York Yankees, 35, 41, 45, 65, 69, 70, 71, 73, 78, 82, 101, 105
Nieman, Bob, 67, 71
Nixon, Richard, 61

Oakland A's, 96, 97, 101
O'Dell, Billy, 69
Ogden, Johnny, 49
opening day: program for, *25;* ticket for, *45*
Oriole motifs, *70, 75, 119*

Oriole Park (formerly Federal League Park), 43, 47, 53, *55*
Orioles Park (formerly Union Park), 13, *17,* 17–18, 21, 24, 27, 31, 36, 43, 47
Orsulak, Joe, 116
Ott, Mel, 81

Palmer, Jim, 13, *13,* 87, 90, 92, 96–101, *100,* 103, 105, 109, 112, 113–14, 126; memorabilia associated with, *100, 101, 115*
Pappas, Milt, 13, 69, 71, 74, 75, 79, 126–27
Parker, Dave, 102
patches, *63, 113, 123*
pennants, *53, 92, 110, 117*
Perez, Tony, 93
Perini, Lou, 58
Perry, Gaylord, 85, 86
Philadelphia Athletics (A's), 40–41, 49, 50
Philadelphia Phillies, 44, 109–12
Philley, Dave, 73
photo packs, *12*
pins, *22, 53, 87, 95*
Pippen, Roger, 58
Pittsburgh Pirates, 20, 96, 102–3
Players League, 19
Portocarrero, Arnold, 69
Powell, Boog, 13, 66, 71, 78, 83, *83,* 90, 92, 93, 94, 99
press passes, *106, 109*
Professional Baseball in America (Dunn), 41
programs, *17, 22, 23, 25, 57, 58, 59, 62, 70;* for All-Star game, *69;* for World Series, *87*

Quinn, Jack, 44

Radio coverage, *57,* 98
reserve clause, 45

INDEX

Rettenmund, Merv, 96
Richards, Paul, 11, 65, *65*, 67, 70, 74
rings: championship, 56, 87, 90, 96, 111, 122
Ripken, Billy, *104*, 115
Ripken, Cal, Jr., 13, *104*, 106, *107*, 108, *108*, 109, 113–16, *121*, 127
Ripken, Cal, Sr., *104*, 114–15
Roberts, Robin, 79
Robinson, Brooks, 13, *66*, 67, 71, 73–79, 81, 83, 87, 90, 92, *93*, 93–94, 96, 103, 117, 128; memorabilia associated with, 76, 77, 95
Robinson, Frank, 11, 12–13, 38, 72, 81–90, *82*, *84*, 92–94, 96, 103, *116*, 128–29; as manager, 115, 116; memorabilia associated with, 84–86
Robinson, Wilbert, 12, 20, 21, 23, 28–29, 31, 32–33, 36
Rockwell, Norman, 77
Roenicke, Gary, 102, 109
Rose, Pete, 93
Russell, Lefty, 41
Ruth, Babe, 12, 41–45, *42*, 47, 81

St. Louis Browns, 23, 41; moved to Baltimore, 58–63, *60*, *62*, 64
San Francisco Giants, 85
Saturday Evening Post, 77
Saverine, Bob, 71
schedules, 57, 58, 59, 62, 67, 68
Schmit, Crazy, 20, 33
Schwalenberg, Greg, 99
scoreboard, *119*
scorebooks, 22, 67, 70, 79
scorecards, 24, 29, 32, 68, 70; for Family Night, 83; for World Series, 87
Seaver, Tom, 90, 92
Segui, David, *121*
Seymour, Cy, 33, 35, 41
Shawkey, Bob, 41

Sheets, Larry, 115
Sherman, Lee, 112–13
Sherman Anti-Trust Act, 45
shoes: of Palmer, 13, 115
Siebold, Socks, 49
signs, 74, 79
Singleton, Ken, 102, 105, 106, *114*
"sketchbooks," 21
Smith, John "Phenomenal," 18
Smith, Nancy, 99
Smith, "Piano Mover," 44
Snyder, Russ, 83
Spanish-American War, 32
Sport, 65
Sporting News, 24–27, *101*
Stargell, Willie, 102
statuettes, *48*, *77*
Stengel, Casey, 68
Stephens, Vern, 63
stock certificate, *16*
Stone, Steve, 105
Suggs, George, 44
Supreme Court, U.S., 45
survey (1954), 66
Swoboda, Ron, 92

Team photos, 14, 18, 25, 30, 42, 46, 52, 54, 103; of Baltimore Premier Athletic Club, 35; of Elite Giants, 39
team portrait, 26
Temple Cup series, 28; of 1897, *17*; program for, *25*
Tenace, Gene, 97
thirtieth-anniversary memorabilia, *113*
Thomas, Tommy, 50
tickets: for All-Star game, 69; for championship series, 92; for opening day, 45; for World Series, 87, 88, 95, 96
Toronto Blue Jays, 116
Triandos, Gus, 67, 68, 75
Triple Crown, 82, 83, 84
Tucker, Tommy, 18, *18*
Turley, Bob, 63, *63*

Uniforms: of Maisel, 44; of mascot/batboy, 10; of Palmer, 13; of Powell, 83. See also jerseys
Union Association, 19
Union Park (later Orioles Park), 13, *17*, 17–18, 21, 24, 27, 31, 36, 43, 47

Van Haltren, George, 20
Veeck, Bill, 58–59
Vickers, Rube, 41
Virginia League, 45
Von Der Horst, Harry, 16, 17–18, 19, 20, 31
Von Der Horst Brewing Co., *17*

Waitkus, Eddie, 61–63
Walsh, Jimmy, 41
Walsh, Runt, 44
Washington Senators, 67
Weaver, Earl, 11, 89, *89*, 90, 96, 97, 101–2, 103, 106, 109, 114, 129
Western Association, 32–33
Westport Stadium, 39
whistle, *99*
White, Roy, 91
Wilhelm, Hoyt, 69, 71
Wilhelm, "Kaiser," 44
Williams, Earl, 97
Williams, Edward Bennett, 105, 112–13
Wilson, Hack, 81
WITH radio, 57, 98
Woodling, Gene, 71, 88
World Series, 11, 57, 76, 97, 101; of 1966, 13, 87, 87–89, *88*; of 1969, 90, 90–92; of 1970, 80, 92–94, *93*, 95; of 1971, 96, *96*; of 1979, 102–3; of 1983, 109–12, *110*, *111*, 113; program for, 87; scorecard for, 87; tickets for, 87, 88, 95, 96

World War I, 47–48
World War II, 79
Worthington, Craig, 115

Yearbooks, 37, 62, 112

Zinn, Guy, 44

PHOTOGRAPHY CREDITS

AP/Wide World Photos: back cover (top left), pp. 66 (bottom right), 78 (top), 80, 82 (both), 88 (top left and bottom right), 89.

Courtesy The Baltimore Sun: p. 55 (bottom).

UPI/Bettmann, New York: p. 60

National Baseball Library & Archive, Cooperstown, New York: pp. 2–3, 14, 17 (bottom), 18–20, 27, 28, 30, 33, 34, 36, 38–40, 42 (top), 46, 49, 51, 52, 62 (top right), 72, 74 (top center), 83 (top left), 84 (top right), 91, 93 (both), 94, 99 (top left), 100 (center), 104, 116.

Jerry Wachter, Baltimore, Maryland/Courtesy National Baseball Library & Archive, Cooperstown, New York: p. 111.

Reprinted by permission of *The Sporting News*: back cover (bottom right), p. 101.

Photo File, Elmsford, New York: front cover (bottom left).